THE DINNER PARTY
PLANNER

Menus and Recipes

In the same series

The Curry Secret
An Indian Housewife's Recipe Book
The Microwave Planner
The Junior Chef
Wholefood For The Whole Family

By the same author

How To Boil An Egg – Simple Cookery For One
No Meat For Me, Please! – Recipes For The Vegetarian
   In The Family

Uniform with this book

THE DINNER PARTY PLANNER

Menus and Recipes

by

Jan Arkless

PAPERFRONTS
ELLIOT RIGHT WAY BOOKS
KINGSWOOD, SURREY, U.K.

Typeset in 10/11½pt Times by County Typesetters, Margate, Kent.

Made and Printed in Great Britain by Richard Clay Ltd., Bungay, Suffolk.

CONTENTS

For Bel's big sister Wizzy,
give simply marvellous dinner parties,
but don't grow up too quickly

1 INTRODUCTION

Enjoy your dinner parties! Remember the emphasis is on entertaining, your guests are coming to enjoy themselves and relax in pleasant company with good food. They are not going to send any dish back, or complain to the head waiter if it's not quite to their liking, nor are they going home to write a gourmet criticism of the evening for the local paper – after all, they're not paying inflated prices for their meal as they might in a far inferior restaurant! A few years ago I enquired of a friend (whom I had invited to Sunday dinner, along with her husband and teenage family) when they would prefer to eat, at lunchtime or in the evening. "When someone else is cooking, I'll eat my Sunday dinner for breakfast if it's more convenient" was the reply! So, relax, try and have everything prepared or under control before your guests arrive, *and if you enjoy yourself your guests will too!*

I'm a great believer in cheating, if it's done circum-spectly! Never deny it if you're found out; boast about it and everyone will wish they'd thought of it first! Mix bought and homemade food if you haven't much time (and you can afford it). I'm not advocating just buying chilled or frozen meals from that well known chain store – good as they are – but a form of 'mix and match'; for example, bought fresh pasta dishes, such as stuffed cannelloni, are lovely, and you can either buy the sauce to serve with it or make a homemade one. If you are desperate, and rich, some of the new posher ready prepared chilled or frozen main courses can mix with your own fresh vegetables (but do make sure the dishes are cooked really thoroughly according to the manufacturer's instructions). Or buy the complete starter, such as a good liver or vegetable pâté, or a gorgeous creamy dessert; always being careful to follow exactly the instructions for storing, defrosting and cooking chilled or frozen food.

Pay attention to the presentation of your dishes, attractive-looking food always tastes better! Garnish soups and sauces by stirring in a swirl of cream or yoghurt; and a sprinkle of parsley or other fresh herbs is impress-ive. A bunch of watercress or a box of mustard and cress is a good standby to strew or bunch on savoury courses for last-minute dressing-up, and the 'aerosol' cream looks good for a final flourish on the pud, although it doesn't really taste quite the same as fresh double cream. Remember it only lasts for a short time too, so don't decorate the mousse until just before serving, or you may be disappointed. Scatter some chopped or flaked nuts, chocolate 'sprinkles' or grated chocolate on top of the cream or a dessert, and there is a wide choice of deliciously different biscuits and wafers to serve with them – a small, expensive packet will go a long way as an accompaniment to a sweet.

I have suggested some specific vegetarian menus, and

there are plenty of recipes for starters and main meals without meat symbolised by a carrot – remember that meat eaters can enjoy vegetarian dishes, but a vegetarian will not be happy if offered meat, although some 'semi-veges' will eat fish. If in doubt, play safe and prepare a meatless meal, using vegetable stock instead of meat stock cubes in the sauces, and not serving any puds containing gelatine. Also take into account foods not eaten by your guests for religious reasons or because of food allergies.

Plan your menu carefully. Choose courses which go together well, but will not all need attention at the last minute, and do as much preparation and cooking as is practical in advance (bearing in mind the need to keep pre-cooked food refrigerated and to reheat it thoroughly, not just warming it through). Planning is the keyword to a successful dinner party, so get as much as possible done beforehand, and then you're not still rushing round in the kitchen as everyone arrives. Set the table early – if you go out to work why not do it the night before? – and put the glasses, china, cutlery, napkins, serving dishes, etc., ready. Sort out flowers and candles if you're going to use them, and put packets of nuts and crisps to hand if you are serving pre-dinner 'nibbles' with the drinks. Find the bottle opener, and put white wine, beers and plenty of mixers, fruit juices and designer water in the fridge, as lots of people are now very aware of the need not to drink at all when driving. If you have a dishwasher, empty it ready for stacking the used dishes after dinner. If you are entertaining on your own, ask one of the guests to help with the drinks, so that you're not trying to dish the food and serve the wine at the same time.

Balance up your courses carefully, mixing rich and plain courses, as no one wants to finish the meal feeling uncomfortable, however delicious the food may have been. Serve a plainer main course between a rich starter and a creamy pud, or a tangy fruit starter before a heavy spicy wine casserole, and off-set richer sauces with plain rice, noodles or vegetables. Take into account variety of shapes, colour and texture when planning the menu – don't have mushroom soup, followed by fish in white sauce followed by rice pudding or crème caramel, as they are too wet, runny and pale-looking when served together, although individually all pleasant, appetising dishes. A sliced tomato and one or two different green or root vegetables will soon brighten up a starter or main course. Don't have too many hot and spicy dishes at the same meal, but on the other hand don't have all very bland ones either as that can be extremely dull; aim for a good mixture of both.

Don't be too ambitious at first if you're new to cooking for a larger number of people; work your menus up gradually. You don't have to serve three courses; two courses are most acceptable, or just a simple main course, such as pasta and salad, followed by a lovely piece of 'posh' cheese – Stilton, Brie (for the brave and greedy!), Roquefort or a special Farmhouse Cheddar – with a beautiful bunch of grapes, fresh bread, biscuits and butter, followed by lots of coffee, all set out attractively, is marvellous, a feast fit for a king, what could be nicer?

I usually serve only one or sometimes two hot courses – it's very reassuring to have the starter and/or pud sitting safely in the fridge by the afternoon. Never have too many dishes that need last-minute attention; a casserole gently bubbling away in the oven and peeled prepared fresh or frozen vegetables ready to be popped on the stove is easy, as is heating up soup or even finishing off a hot meringue pudding (but hopefully not all for the same dinner!), but you don't want to be preparing a hot starter, making a sauce for the main course, peeling veg and whipping the cream as your guests arrive. A lot of the recipes in this book can be prepared in advance the day before or in the morning, and kept chilled in the fridge, and will then only require putting into the oven at the calculated time or just putting onto the table. Some dishes (symbolised by a snowflake), can be prepared further in advance and frozen, if you have the time and a freezer, but remember to take them from the freezer in time to defrost before cooking. As a general rule it's better to cook food only once, so if possible chill or freeze dishes uncooked, these stages are suggested in the recipes too.

Wash and prepare fresh vegetables in advance and leave them ready to cook in the saucepan, or make one of the delicious potato or vegetable dishes that can be left to cook slowly in the oven, and which doesn't mind waiting if your guests are late. Fresh and frozen vegetables can be quickly cooked at the last minute, and are best slightly undercooked if you are going to keep them warm while everyone is eating the first course, (see Chapter 6). Pasta, instead of potato, is quick and easy to cook at the last minute, and rice can be cooked and kept warm until needed without going 'puddingy' if slightly undercooked too. A large bowl of fresh salad, either a plain green salad or a mixed one with lots of the different lettuces, vegetables and fruit now available (you only need a small amount of each to make a big bowl of salad), is the easy way out. Make the dressing in advance too, but don't mix them until just before serving or the lettuce will go limp. A cold rice salad is even better, as it can be made and mixed with the dressing in advance, to give the rice time to absorb the flavour of the dressing. Hot puddings are mostly very good tempered and can be pre-cooked and warmed gently or cooked from cold while you are eating the main course – I must admit I prefer the peace of mind of pre-cooking, it's less nerve-racking!

Write out your complete menu – including sauces, accompaniments and trimmings – and juggle it about until you're happy with it. There are suggested menus in Chapter 2, ranging from the fairly cheap and easy to more expensive ideas for the more experienced cook, (if you want Cordon Bleu recipes I'm sure you have your own ideas anyway) and vegetable accompaniments are also suggested with each main course. All the recipes for these menus, including potatoes, pasta or rice, vegetables and sauces, are to be found in the appropriate sections, so that it will be easy to plan your own menus from these sections too. Of course you can change and substitute any of the starters and puds, but do check that you haven't left yourself too much to do at the last minute.

Whatever menu you choose, calculate cooking and reheating times to make sure everything will be ready when you want to eat, bearing in mind that guests are often a little late, and that you will want some time for drinks and chat before you sit down. Write out a timetable under your menu for preparing and cooking dishes, including times for putting each dish into the oven or the saucepan onto the stove, and keep it handy to use on the day – I stick my menu and timetable behind a cupboard door and cross off each dish as it's finished, that way nothing gets forgotten or left behind in the fridge. I also like to write out a shopping list and check the contents of the store cupboard against the recipes – you don't want to find you've run out of cornflour or gravy powder at the vital moment you need them. Check that you have the cooking and serving dishes necessary for your chosen menu, especially if you're serving several courses – you can't use the ramekins for a hot starter if you've already got a cold dessert waiting in them!

I prefer to get everything cooked and dished into serving dishes before the guests are due (with slightly undercooked veg so that they don't go soggy), then I keep them hot in my 'horrible hostess' as my youngest son called it when it was first purchased, as he didn't think the serving dishes were large enough. However, we've often been ten for supper or Sunday dinner and I don't think he's gone hungry yet! If you entertain a lot I would certainly recommend a heated trolley, hot cupboard or hot tray, as they really do keep the food at the correct temperature and leave the oven clear for other dishes. Otherwise, put dishes of hot food into a very, very low oven (100°C/200°F/gas ½–1) to keep it hot, or reheat it in a microwave, following the manufacturer's instructions implicitly.

My ultimate aim with every dinner party is to be washed and changed, make up and hair done, the whole meal dished and ready to serve, five minutes before the guests are due, so that I can sit smugly in happy anticipation of a super evening, enjoying that first marvellous glass of sherry or gin and tonic, before the doorbell rings!

P.S. – I don't always manage it, but it's fun trying!

Following the recipes

All the menus and recipes should serve six people with good appetites – bearing in mind that if you are entertaining four or five huge and hearty members of the rugby team you may need larger quantities of food than you would prepare for three couples. Reduce the amounts given in the recipes by a third if you're serving four people, but it's always better to have plenty of food than not enough, so if there are only going to be five of you I'd play safe and use the recipes as they are; you can always eat up the left-overs next day. There's nothing more embarrassing than watching everyone being polite and only taking minute helpings, or, even worse, running out of a particular dish before everyone is served. Obviously if you are serving several different vegetables you can reduce the amount of each variety, but if you are offering a choice of puds you can be sure that everyone will want to try a little of each, so cater accordingly.

There is a section of recipes for each course – Cold Beginnings and Hot Starters, Simply Super and Posher Nosh main courses, Proper Puds and Dreamy Desserts. Each section starts with simple recipes, leading up to the more expensive dishes, although there is nothing too outrageous or difficult to make. There are also some complete Vegetarian menus, and the other cold and hot starters and main courses acceptable to vegetarians are symbolised by a carrot. All the puds and desserts can be eaten happily by vegetarians (unless they're slimming!). Amounts to use and methods of cooking potatoes, pasta, rice, fresh and frozen vegetables and potato and vegetable dishes are covered in separate sections. Suitable 'fillers' – potatoes, pasta, rice or bread – and vegetable accompaniments are suggested with each main course recipe. There are symbols by each starter and main course recipe to help with your meal planning:

⬛ – serve hot

⬛ – serve cold

⬛ – actual preparation and/or cooking requiring attention at the last minute

⬛ – *very* simple (nothing in this book is very difficult!)

⬛ – can be prepared and frozen beforehand, then served frozen or defrosted to cook

⬛ – suitable for vegetarians

Most of the recipes can be prepared beforehand (the night before or on the day) and can then be garnished and served cold or put aside until it's time to put in the oven. Any recipes which need actual last minute attention are symbolised by the letters "LM".

Homemade dishes which have been frozen should usually be defrosted before cooking or reheating, so the night before a dinner party I take most of the pre-prepared dishes from the freezer and leave them to defrost overnight – it's safer than forgetting a vital dish and being faced with a solid lump of casserole or pud just before you need to use it. Small or thin items, such as garlic bread, or cold puds ready to eat, will defrost the same day and can be removed from the freezer in the morning. Once defrosted, treat everything like fresh food and store in the fridge or a cool place until needed.

Preparation times, cooking times and reheating times (where appropriate) are given with the recipes, as well as suggested methods of preparing and storing dishes in advance, so that once you've made the dish (or defrosted it if pre-prepared) you only have to calculate the time for putting the food in the oven or the pan on the stove according to the planned eating time, in order to have everything ready together. If your maths are as dodgy as mine, double check your sums, then write out your whole menu and timetable, stick it to the cupboard door and you're ready to go. The suggested menus have all been planned for easy preparation and presentation, with courses that go well together, so that you can produce a lovely complete meal, with everything ready (seemingly effortlessly to your guests!) at the right time, without the panic of having to do everything at once at the last minute.

I'm assuming that most people contemplating entertaining have access to a kitchen with basic kitchen equipment. You may not have everything in the suggested list below, (you probably have your own favourite utensils and gadgets anyway), but this is a list of equipment which I have found useful. I'm not really a 'gadget person' so it's not very long! If you don't have any large cooking or serving dishes and can't borrow them or don't want to go to the expense of buying large dishes for only very occasional use, there are plenty of foil dishes in varying sizes available quite cheaply from supermarkets or freezer shops. An electric mixer, a liquidizer or blender or a food processor are certainly very useful – they don't have to be large and expensive. I've catered for years for a family of six plus friends with a small mixer and blender; and a handheld electric mixer is not much dearer than a good quality egg beater. You will find a mixer and blender of some kind very handy in quite a few of the recipes.

Useful Equipment

Chopping board
Cling film
Colander and/or sieve
Cooking foil
Cooking tongs
Electric mixer or
    egg beater or
    food processor
Fish slice
Grater
Kitchen paper
Kitchen scales

Kitchen scissors
Liquidizer or blender
    or food processor
Measuring jug
Potato masher
Potato peeler
Pie slice – for serving
Rolling pin
Salad shaker or spinner
Serrated bread knife
Sharp cook's knife for
    meat etc.
Sharp vegetable knife
Slotted spoon

Dishes – suitable sizes for six, and these are the sizes called 'large ovenproof dish' etc. in the recipes:

Large casserole – the kind that can go on top of the stove or in the oven: 5–6½ pint/3–3½ litre.

1 or 2 deep ovenproof dishes – in ovenproof glass or pottery: 2–3″/5–7½cm deep and 2½–3½ pint/1½–2 litre capacity, with or without lids.

Ovenproof pie dish: 2½–3 pint/1–1½ litre.

Ovenproof pie plate: 9–10″/23–25cm.

Ovenproof flan dish: 9–10″/23–25cm.

6 ovenproof ramekin dishes.
6 sundae, cocktail or large wine glasses – use for starters and cold desserts.

Desirable Extras
Heated trolley, hot cupboard or hot tray.
Microwave oven – useful for defrosting and last-minute cooking or reheating.
Freezer.

This list looks formidable, but you won't need everything, and you probably have most of the items already.

Abbreviations
In the recipes, tsp = teaspoon; tblsp = tablespoon; mins. = minutes.

COOKERY TERMS
Al dente – referring to vegetables, pasta or rice that is cooked but feels firm when bitten.
Folding – careful combining of two ingredients (one of which is usually whipped up, e.g. egg white or cream), in order to mix them together without breaking the air bubbles. Usually done with a metal spoon.
To glaze – brushing with milk and/or egg to give a golden brown, shiny finish when cooking pastry, or coating meat with a sauce to give a shiny, crisp coating.
Knock up – *in cookery* this means pinching together the edges of a pastry crust and then trimming and cutting with a knife to make a neat edge.
Par boil – to partly cook food (usually fresh vegetables) in boiling water for a few minutes, before finishing cooking by some other method.
Rub in – rubbing flour and fat (butter, margarine, lard or vegetable fat) together between the finger tips, until it mixes roughly together and resembles fresh breadcrumbs.

Reduce – to boil juices or sauces quite hard for a few minutes to allow some of the liquid to evaporate.

Warm plates (essential for a hot meal) – either by putting them into a warm oven or hot trolley, or warming above the stove on a plate rack, or by leaving them in the washing-up bowl covered by very hot water for a few minutes.

2   SUGGESTED MENUS

Each menu consists of three courses that go well together to make a lovely meal. The dishes can be prepared in advance, leaving the minimum of last-minute finishing when your guests arrive.

The timetables will provide a simple guide to preparation times, assuming that you only have one oven in which to cook and keep everything warm. If you have a double oven, heated trolley or hot plate, life is easier as you can cook dishes and keep them warm, without having to get everything ready at the last minute.

The suggested potatoes, vegetables and other accompaniments are easy to prepare with the main course, but can be changed to suit your own taste, budget or what is in season according to the time of year. A choice of potato and/or vegetable dish cooked in the oven and fresh or frozen vegetables are suggested where appropriate – for goodness sake don't try to serve all of them! – and, of course, you can substitute your own choice of starters and puds from the recipes in the following chapters, but be careful not to choose courses that all require last-minute attention while your guests are waiting.

Finish the meal with a tempting cheese board (prepared in advance) as well as, or instead of, dessert (if you wish), and lots of fresh coffee or tea – designer teas, Earl Grey, Jasmine, Lemon, Camomile, etc., are becoming extremely popular – and those lovely chocolate crisps or mints. Get it all ready when you set the table.

In the timetables, I am assuming that the guests are invited for 8 o'clock, which means they should all have arrived by 8.30 p.m., and you will actually sit down to eat about 9 p.m. Set the table and put plates and serving dishes ready to warm and use beforehand.

SIMPLY SUPER

Menu 1

Easy, cheap and very cheerful.

Honeymoon Melon Boats with Orange Sails (p. 107)

* * *

Beef or Vegetable Lasagne (p. 46)

Green/Mixed Salad   Vinaigrette Dressing

Hot French Bread or Rolls and Butter

* * *

Ice-Cream with Chocolate Fudge Sauce (p. 132)

The week before: Prepare chosen Bolognese sauce and

freeze; or make and freeze complete lasagne, uncooked.

Prepare vinaigrette dressing, store in fridge.

The night before: Take Bolognese or lasagne from freezer.

On the day: Prepare complete lasagne if not pre-cooked, store uncooked in fridge.

Make chocolate fudge sauce, leave in pyrex jug. Put chosen toppings, cream and biscuits ready.

Prepare melon, chill in fridge. Make salad, take dressing from fridge. Put butter on serving dish.

7.45: Heat the oven at 180°C/350°F/gas 4–5.

8.10: Put lasagne on top oven shelf to cook.

8.50: Check lasagne: put on lower shelf if cooked, or leave for a further few minutes. Toss salad in dressing.

Stand jug of chocolate sauce in a pan with 2″/5cm hot water and leave over a low heat to reheat.

Put bread or rolls in oven on top shelf.

9.00: Dish hot bread. Serve melon. Warm plates.

Lower oven heat to 100°C/200°F/gas ½–1 and leave main course to keep warm while eating starter.

Menu 2   V

With the 'hot' main course, serve a cold starter and
a reviving chilled dessert.

Avocado – filling of choice (p. 110–112)

* * *

Chilli con Carne or Vegetable Chilli (p. 49–50)

Jacket Potatoes   Green/Mixed Salad   Yoghurt Dressing

Garlic Bread or Rolls and Butter

* * *

Tangarine Dessert (p. 132) with Cream or Greek Yoghurt

The week before: Make double quantity of chosen Bolognese sauce and freeze.

Prepare garlic bread and freeze.

The night before: Prepare tangarine dessert and leave to chill in fridge.

Take Bolognese sauce from freezer.

On the day: Take garlic bread from freezer or make garlic bread if not pre-frozen.

Make Bolognese sauce if not pre-frozen. Scrub potatoes, wrap in foil if liked. Prepare salad.

Make yoghurt dressing, store in fridge. Spoon syrup over prepared dessert. Put cream or Greek yoghurt into a dish, leave in fridge. Put butter on serving dish.

Prepare avocado, leave in fridge.

6.45: Heat the oven at 200°C/400°F/gas 6–7.

7.00 approx. (according to preferred method of cooking): Put jacket potatoes in oven to bake, timed to be ready about 8.55.

8.40: Reheat chilli over a low heat, simmering very gently for 5–10 minutes to make sure it's really hot before serving.

Heat garlic bread in oven.

8.55: Turn oven down to 100°C/200°F/gas ½–1.

Put potatoes into a dish, keep warm. Put chilli in a dish, keep warm.

Leave garlic bread in oven, pop bread rolls in oven to warm slightly. Warm plates. Toss salad in dressing.

9.00: Serve avocado.

Menu 3

Deliciously different and so easy to prepare.
Substitute any cold starter if you prefer it.

Lettuce Soup (p. 119)

* * *

Norwegian Special – Fresh Prawns (p. 50)

Potato Salad   Mixed Salad with Dressing

Garlic Bread or Rolls and Butter

* * *

Raspberry or Strawberry Cream (p. 135)

The week before: Make garlic bread and freeze.
Make vinaigrette dressing, store in fridge.
The night before: Make lettuce soup and store in fridge
ready to reheat, or leave to chill if serving cold.
On the day: Remove garlic bread from freezer.
Prepare raspberry/strawberry cream, dish up and store
in fridge. Make potato salad and put aside.
Make mixed salad, remove salad dressing from fridge
and put aside.
Prepare prawns, put in serving glasses and store in
fridge.
Put mayonnaise in serving dish or make avocado sauce
and put in dish.
Make croûtons, put aside on kitchen paper, wash
parsley for garnish (find the scissors ready for later), put
cream or yoghurt ready for soup. Wash mint sprigs to
decorate pudding.
8.45: Heat the oven at 200°C/400°F/gas 6–7 for garlic
bread.
Put soup plates to warm. Heat soup gently and simmer
for 5 minutes to make sure it's really hot.
Toss salad in dressing. Heat water for fingerbowls if
used. Put garlic bread in hot oven.
9.00: Dish out and garnish hot or cold soup and serve.
Don't forget the garlic bread is in the oven!

Menu 4

An unusual light starter with a tasty, easy
casserole and a hot pud.

Fruit Salad Savoury (p. 112)

* * *

Tomato Braised Steak (p. 51)

Scalloped Potatoes (p. 85)   Jacket Potatoes

Cauliflower/Broccoli   Swede   Frozen Peas

* * *

Bread and Butter Pudding with Cream (p. 126)

The week before: Prepare and freeze tomato braised
steak.
The night before: Take braised steak from freezer.
On the day: Prepare fruit salad savoury and put in fridge,
wash herbs for garnish.

Prepare tomato braised steak if not pre-frozen, and
leave in fridge.

Prepare scalloped potatoes or scrub jacket potatoes.
Prepare chosen fresh vegetables.

Make and cook bread and butter pudding, put aside
until needed. Dish up cream.
6.15: Heat the oven at 170°C/350°F/gas 3–4.
6.30: Put tomato braised steak in oven to cook.
7.00: Turn oven up to 200°C/400°F/gas 6–7, put braised
steak on bottom shelf (not the floor) of the oven.

Put scalloped potatoes or jacket potatoes on top shelf
(adjust times according to dish size and method of cooking
jacket potatoes).
8.30: Cook fresh vegetables.

8.45: Cook frozen vegetables.
  Adjust seasoning in casserole, check potatoes.
  Turn oven down low to 100°C/200°F/gas ½–1.
  Drain, mash and put swede in a dish, keep warm.
  Drain and put vegetables in a dish, keep warm.
  Warm plates.
8.55: Dish out and garnish fruit salad savoury.
9.00: Serve starter.

When main course is served, pop bread and butter pudding into oven (170°C/325°F/gas 3–4) to warm through for 10–15 minutes – don't forget it while eating!

Menu 5

A lovely, warming winter menu, but check that you have room in the oven for all the dishes, otherwise choose vegetables that can be cooked on top of the stove.

Stuffed Tomato Cups (p. 113)

*   *   *

Pork in Cider Sauce (p. 53)

Herb Scalloped Potatoes   *Creamed/New Potatoes*

Savoury Red Cabbage (p. 99)   *French/Runner Beans*
Broccoli/Broad Beans

*   *   *

Hot Peach Crunch (p. 125)   *Cream or Greek Yoghurt*

The week before: Prepare and freeze pork in cider.
The night before: Take pork in cider from freezer.
On the day: Prepare pork in cider if not pre-frozen, and leave uncooked in fridge. Wash parsley for garnish.
  Prepare hot peach crunch, put aside ready to bake.
  Prepare herb scalloped potatoes or peel or scrub

creamed or new potatoes, and leave in cold water until needed.

Prepare savoury red cabbage, put aside.

Prepare fresh vegetables, put aside.

Prepare tomato cups, put in fridge.

Dish up cream for pudding, leave in fridge.

6.30: Heat the oven at 200°C/400°F/gas 6–7.

6.45: Put herb scalloped potatoes on top shelf.

Put peach crunch on bottom shelf.

7.10ish: Remove cooked pud and put aside.

Put savoury red cabbage on lower shelf.

7.30: Put pork in cider in oven on shelf above red cabbage (with potato dish).

8.30: Cook creamed or new potatoes.

8.40: Cook fresh and frozen vegetables.

Check casseroles: if cooked, lower oven heat to 100°C/200°F/gas ½–1.

Drain and prepare creamed potatoes, dish and keep warm; or drain and dish new potatoes, keep warm. Drain and dish vegetables and keep warm.

Warm plates.

9.00: Serve tomato cups.

After serving main course, pop the hot peach crunch back into the oven, on the top shelf, to warm through again.

Menu 6

A substantial starter and main course are offset
with plain vegetables and a light pudding.

Ham and Asparagus Mornay (p. 122)

* * *

Goulash (p. 54) with Noodles

Green/Mixed Salad   Vinaigrette Dressing

Courgettes   Carrots   Frozen Peas

* * *

Pears in Red Wine (p. 124)   Cream

The week before: Prepare ham and asparagus mornay, freeze uncooked.

Prepare, cook and freeze goulash.

Make vinaigrette and store in fridge.

The night before: Take mornay and goulash from freezer.

On the day: Prepare goulash if not made in advance, cook in the oven (170°C/325°F/gas 3–4) for 2–2½ hours, adding the potatoes after 1¼ hours, and the mushrooms for the last 15 minutes.

Prepare pears in red wine, cook in the oven with the goulash for 1–1¼ hours, then put aside or chill in fridge as preferred.

Prepare ham and asparagus mornay if not pre-prepared, leave uncooked in fridge.

Prepare salad, put aside. Take dressing from fridge but do not mix.

Prepare fresh vegetables, put aside. Weigh noodles, put chosen garnish ready. Put cream into serving dish.

8.00: Heat the oven at 200°C/400°F/gas 6–7.

8.15: Put ham and asparagus mornay on top shelf of oven to cook.

Put goulash on lower shelf of oven to heat through.

8.30: Cook vegetables. Toss salad in dressing.

Cook noodles.

8.50: Check goulash and mornay, lower oven heat to 100°C/200°F/gas ½-1. Warm plates.

Drain vegetables, put in a dish and keep warm.

Drain noodles, put in a dish, garnish, keep hot.

9.00: Serve the starter.

If serving pears in red wine as a hot dish, after serving main course, turn oven up to 170°C/325°F/gas 3–4, and put pears in oven until needed.

Menu 7

Panic dinner – inspired by my son Jonathan's super instant entertaining. Buy on the way home from work, and assemble in minutes!

Melon (p. 106) – plain, with sorbet or Parma ham or Bought Liver/Vegetable Pâté with Hot Toast

* * *

Cheating Cannelloni (p. 56) – Bought or Home-made Tomato Sauce
Mixed Green Salad   Vinaigrette Dressing
Garlic/French Bread or Granary Rolls   Butter

* * *

Brandy Snaps with Cream (page 134)

The week before: Prepare and freeze tomato sauce.
Make vinaigrette and store in fridge.
The night before: Take tomato sauce from freezer.
On the day: Defrost garlic bread, or buy ready frozen, or make fresh if time.

Prepare cannelloni, leave in fridge, leave extra sauce in saucepan.

Prepare melon, and Parma ham if used, chill in fridge. If filling melon with sorbet, the sorbet must be scooped into the prepared melon 'cups' just before serving.

Or slice chosen pâté onto plates and garnish with a little salad. Slice bread ready for toast (or use a sliced loaf), put butter into a dish and leave out to soften.

Put brandy snaps ready. Whip cream until very stiff and put in fridge.

8.00: Heat the oven at 180°C/350°F/gas 4–5.

8.15: Put cannelloni in oven, covered with foil.

8.40: Remove foil lid from cannelloni.

Put garlic bread in oven to heat. Dress salad.

Make toast, serve wrapped loosely in a napkin to keep it warm. Heat extra sauce gently in saucepan.

8.55: Lower oven heat to 100°C/200°F/gas ½–1. Warm plates. Put bread rolls in oven to warm and leave main course in oven to keep warm.

9.00: Serve starter.

Quickly fill brandy snaps with cream after eating main course, arrange on a dish and serve.

POSHER NOSH

Menu 1

An unusual casserole in a rich sauce, but very good natured: it doesn't mind waiting if your guests are a little late.

Baked Eggs (p. 122)

* * *

Pork and Beansprout Casserole (p. 58)

Noodles/Jacket Potatoes   French/Runner Beans

Broccoli/Cauliflower

* * *

Citrus Cheesecake (p. 138) Cream or Greek Yoghurt

The week before: Prepare, cook and freeze pork and beansprout casserole (see recipe).

Make and freeze citrus cheesecake.

The night before: Take casserole from freezer.

On the day: Take cheesecake from freezer or prepare cheesecake and store in fridge. Put the cream in a dish and store in fridge.

Make casserole if not pre-frozen, and partly cook (see recipe).

Weigh noodles and put ready, or scrub potatoes.

Prepare fresh vegetables, put aside. Prepare baked eggs, put uncooked in ramekins in fridge.

6.30: Heat the oven at 180°C/350°F/gas 4–5.

6.45: Put jacket potatoes in oven.

8.00: Finish casserole (see recipe) and put in oven to reheat.

8.30: Stir casserole. Cook fresh or frozen vegetables. Cook pasta.

8.45: Check casserole and potatoes, put on lower shelf.

Put baked eggs on top oven shelf.

Warm plates (put them in hot water if you've no room in the oven).

Drain, dish and garnish vegetables, keep them warm.

Drain, dish and garnish pasta, keep warm.

Dish jacket potatoes, keep warm.

9.00: Turn oven down to 100°C/200°F/gas ½–1.

Serve baked eggs.

Menu 2

One of my son Ki's favourite menus, so it must be good!

Tomato Salad (p. 103)   Rolls and Butter

* * *

Chicken in Crunchy Peanut Sauce (p. 61)
Ki's Special Potatoes (p. 88)   Creamed/New Potatoes
Broccoli   Carrot Sticks   Mangetout Peas

* * *

Apple Snow (p. 137)

The week before: Prepare apple purée and freeze.

The night before: Take apple purée from freezer.

On the day: Make apple purée if not pre-frozen, prepare apple snow, dish it up and put in fridge.

Prepare chicken in peanut sauce, put in fridge until time to cook.

Prepare Ki's potatoes, put aside. Peel or scrub old or new potatoes, leave in cold water.

Prepare chosen vegetables, put aside.

Prepare tomato salad, dish and put aside.

Put butter on serving dish.

6.30: Heat the oven at 200°C/400°F/gas 6–7.

6.45: Put Ki's potatoes in oven, on top shelf.

7.30 or 8.00: Put chicken casserole into oven below potatoes – check recipe for cooking times.

8.30: Stir sweetcorn into casserole.

Cook new or creamed potatoes.

Cook fresh or frozen vegetables.

8.45: Check Ki's potatoes and chicken, turn oven down to 100°C/200°F/gas ½–1. Put rolls in oven to warm.

Warm plates. Drain, cream and dish potatoes; or drain and dish new potatoes, keep warm.

Drain and dish vegetables, keep warm.

9.00: Put warm rolls in a dish and serve tomato salad.

Menu 3

Do check beforehand that everyone likes fish or you've got problems. Choose a nice selection of vegetables from those suggested in the menu.

Chicken Bouchées (p. 118)

* * *

Herb Stuffed Fish Steaks (p. 62)
(continued overleaf)

(Menu 3 continued)

Pommes Boulanger (p. 87)   *Potato/Parsnip Castles*

New/Boiled Potatoes   *Courgette & Tomato Bake (p. 97)*

Green Beans   *Broccoli*   *Peas*

* * *

Mum's Chocolate Mousse (p. 139)
Cream or Crème Fraiche

The week before: The bouchée cases may be cooked and frozen if you're going to be rushed on the day, but they're fragile when cooked, so store in a lidded plastic box.

Prepare and freeze stuffing.

Prepare and freeze potato/parsnip castles.

The night before: Take stuffing from freezer.

On the day: Take bouchée cases from freezer.

Take potato/parsnip castles from freezer.

Bake bouchée cases if not pre-frozen.

Put chicken sauce in pan ready to heat, store in fridge, and prepare garnish.

Prepare stuffing if not pre-frozen, prepare fish steaks for cooking, and put in fridge.

Prepare pommes boulanger, put aside. Prepare potato/parsnip castles if not pre-frozen, put aside.

Scrub or peel new or boiled potatoes, leave in cold water.

Prepare courgette & tomato bake, put aside.

Prepare chosen vegetables, put aside.

Make chocolate mousse, dish and put in fridge; dish up cream, put in fridge.

6.30: Heat the oven at 200°C/400°F/gas 6–7.

6.45: Put pommes boulanger in oven (top shelf).

8.10: Put fish in oven below potatoes.

Put courgette bake in oven on lower shelf.

8.30: Put potato/parsnip castles in oven on top shelf.
Cook fresh and frozen vegetables.
8.45: Check dishes in oven. Put potatoes on oven floor and heat pastry cases on top shelf for 3–5 minutes.
Heat plates for starters.
Drain and dish vegetables, keep warm.
Heat chicken sauce over very gentle heat, season and add herbs. Put pastry cases onto serving plates and finish starters.
Lower oven heat to 100°C/200°F/gas ½–1 and put plates in oven to warm.
9.00: Serve starter.

Menu 4

A traditional Sunday dinner, but you can enjoy it any time. There is a choice of puddings in case you don't have a freezer.

Citrus Cocktail (p. 106)

* * *

Roast Pork (p. 64)

Mix 'n Match Stuffing (p. 147)   *Apple Sauce (p. 152)*

Roast Potatoes   Roast Parsnips   Roast Onions

Boiled or New Potatoes   Cabbage or Brussels Sprouts

Carrots   Cauliflower   Frozen Peas   Gravy

* * *

Crunchy Apple and Blackberry Ice-Cream (p. 140)

or Sunshine Pie (p. 128)   Cream or Greek Yoghurt

The week before: Make and freeze stuffing.
Make and freeze apple sauce.

Make and freeze ice-cream and sunshine pie.

The night before: Take stuffing from freezer.

Take apple sauce from freezer.

Peel potatoes, leave in cold water. Peel parsnips, leave in cold water with a little lemon juice.

Prepare fresh vegetables, leave in saucepans in a cool place.

On the day: Take sunshine pie from freezer.

Make citrus cocktail, chill in fridge, rinse mint or lemon balm for garnish.

Make and bake sunshine pie if not pre-frozen, dish up cream or yoghurt.

Prepare stuffing and apple sauce if not pre-frozen, put aside. Prepare potatoes and vegetables if not done last night.

Mix gravy, ready to add water and cook.

Prepare joint, put in roasting tin.

6.15: Heat the oven at 200°C/400°F/gas 6–7.

6.30: Put joint in oven.

7.00: Check joint, cover with foil if crackling is crisp enough. Put stuffing in oven.

7.30: Par boil potatoes and parsnips, heat fat in roasting tin.

7.40: Put stuffing to keep warm (use oven floor if necessary), drain potatoes and parsnips and put in hot baking tin. Put onions in roasting tin – the vegetables can be cooked round the meat if liked.

8.00: Turn potatoes, parsnips and onions to brown both sides, turn meat over.

8.30: Take ice-cream from freezer, leave to soften.

Cook new or boiled potatoes.

Cook fresh and frozen vegetables.

Heat apple sauce gently in saucepan, and put in a dish, or heat on oven floor.

8.45: Put the meat on a dish, leave to stand in a warm place, covered with foil.

Dish potatoes, parsnips and onions, and keep warm.

Turn oven down to 100°C/200°F/gas ½–1.

Drain, dish and garnish boiled or new potatoes (save water for gravy) keep hot. Drain, dish and garnish vegetables, save water for gravy, keep hot.

Warm plates. Finish gravy, using meat juices and vegetable water, leave in saucepan.

8.55: Dish and garnish citrus cocktail.

9.00: Serve starter. Reheat gravy before serving.

When main course is served, put the sunshine pie into the low oven to warm through until needed.

Check ice-cream, and when soft enough, put into fridge until needed.

Menu 5

Impress foreign visitors and all your British
friends with gourmet English cooking ('burnt cream'
is the English name for the pud).

Garlic Mushrooms (p. 121)

* * *

Steak and Kidney Pie (p. 66)

Onion Scalloped Potatoes (p. 87)

Boiled/New/Roast Potatoes

Savoury Red Cabbage   Cauliflower

Cabbage/Broccoli   Peas   Gravy

* * *

Tim's Crème Brûlée (p. 142)

The week before: Prepare and freeze complete steak and kidney pie (do not cook) and freeze pie filling.

Freeze extra gravy.

The day before: Prepare crème brûlée, leave in fridge.

Take pie filling and gravy from freezer.

On the day: Take complete pie from freezer, or cook pie filling and prepare pie. Put in fridge.

Prepare onion scalloped potatoes. Peel or scrub potatoes for boiled/new/roast potatoes, leave in cold water.

Prepare savoury red cabbage.

Prepare fresh vegetables, put aside.

Prepare and cook garlic mushrooms, put aside. Slice bread ready for toast, rinse herbs for garnish. Finish gravy ready for cooking.

In the afternoon: Finish crème brûlée, return to fridge.

6.30: Heat the oven at 200°C/400°F/gas 6–7.

6.45: Put onion scallops on top shelf to cook.

Put savoury red cabbage on lower shelf.

7.30: Put fat in roasting tin to heat, par boil roast potatoes, drain and put in oven on top shelf.

8.15: Take red cabbage from oven, keep warm.

Put pie on top shelf (move potatoes down).

8.30: Put boiled/new potatoes to cook. Cook fresh and frozen vegetables.

8.45: Check pie and scalloped potatoes, turn oven down to 100°C/200°F/gas ½–1.

Drain and dish boiled/new potatoes and vegetables, garnish and keep warm, save water for gravy. Warm plates. Finish gravy, leave in saucepan.

8.55: Make toast, heat garlic mushrooms and finish starter.

9.00: Serve starter.

Reheat gravy just before serving main course.

Menu 6

A different and trouble-free roast dinner.

Grilled Grapefruit (p. 118)

*   *   *

Roast Beef in Vegetable Gravy (p. 68)

Yorkshire Puddings (p. 70)

Roast Potatoes   *New/Boiled Potatoes*

Jacket Potatoes   *Green Salad*

French/Runner Beans   *Brussels Sprouts*   *Peas*

*   *   *

Apple Tart (p. 127)   *Cream or Greek Yoghurt*

The week before: Prepare and freeze apple tart (raw or cooked as you prefer). Make vinaigrette.

The night before: Take apple tart from freezer.

On the day: Prepare and cook apple tart if not pre-cooked and frozen, put aside.

Prepare beef in vegetable gravy, put in roasting tin and put aside.

Make Yorkshire pudding mix, leave in fridge.

Peel potatoes, leave in cold water, or scrub jacket potatoes.

Prepare green salad, put aside, take vinaigrette dressing from fridge.

Prepare fresh vegetables, put aside.

Dish up cream or yoghurt, leave in fridge.

Prepare grapefruit, leave ready to toast in grill pan.

7.00: Heat the oven at 200°C/400°F/gas 6–7.

7.15ish: Put jacket potatoes in oven.

Put beef and vegetable gravy in oven.

7.30: Put fat to heat in roasting tin, par boil roast potatoes, drain and put in hot fat in the oven on the top shelf.

8.25: Heat fat in tins for Yorkshire puds; these must go on the top shelf, so you may have to do some juggling about.

8.30: Put Yorkshire puds in to cook. Put new/boiled potatoes on to cook. Cook fresh and frozen vegetables.

8.45:   Drain potatoes, dish and keep warm.

Drain vegetables, dish and keep warm.

Turn oven down to 100°C/200°F/gas ½–1.

Dish jacket or roast potatoes, keep warm.

Dish Yorkshire puds and keep warm. Dish beef, leave to stand on serving dish, covered with foil.

Thicken gravy – you will have to do this on the top of the stove if you are using the oven to keep things warm, otherwise leave oven temperature on high and put roasting tin of thickened gravy back in hot oven for 5–10 minutes until cooked.

Heat grill, toast grapefruit.

9.00: Serve grapefruit.

The gravy should be reheated just before serving, or dished up straight from the oven. Put apple tart into a low oven (150°C/300°F/gas 2–3) to warm gently while eating main course.

Menu 7

An impressive meal, but easy to prepare in advance, needing a minimum of last-minute attention.

Potted Shrimps (p. 115)

* * *

Sticky Roast Gammon with Pineapple (p. 71)

Jacket/Stuffed Jacket Potatoes (p. 84–85)

Roast/New Potatoes   *Mushrooms à la Grecque (p. 98)*

Broccoli/Cauliflower   Mangetout/Peas
Pineapple Gravy

* * *

Citrus Cheesecake (p. 138) Cream or Greek Yoghurt

The week before: Make and freeze citrus cheesecake.

The night before: Prepare stuffed jacket potatoes, leave in fridge. Soak gammon for appropriate time, dry and leave in fridge.

On the day: Take cheesecake from freezer or prepare cheesecake and leave in fridge.

Prepare potted shrimps and leave in fridge; put bread or rolls ready and butter on serving dish.

Partly cook gammon joint in foil, glaze and put aside – see recipe. Scrub jacket potatoes if not prepared the night before, peel or scrub roast/new potatoes, leave in cold water.

Prepare mushrooms à la Grecque, put aside.

Prepare fresh vegetables.

Prepare gravy mix and put aside.

7.00: Heat the oven at 200°C/400°F/gas 6–7.

7.15: Put jacket potatoes in to cook.

7.45: Par boil roast potatoes – cook for about 15 minutes so that they can just finish off round the gammon.

8.00: Put gammon in to roast, leave for 5 minutes until fat is hot, then put potatoes in to roast.

Put mushrooms à la Grecque to cook on lower shelf.

8.30: Cook new potatoes.

Heat stuffed jacket potatoes on top shelf, put gammon onto lower shelf and mushrooms onto floor of oven.

Cook fresh and frozen vegetables.

Put pineapple round gammon to heat.

8.45: Check dishes in oven, reduce oven heat to 100°C/200°F/gas ½–1, dish gammon, cover with foil and leave to stand in a warm place.

Dish jacket/stuffed jacket potatoes, keep warm.

Garnish mushrooms, keep warm.

Drain and dish new potatoes, keep warm.

Drain and dish vegetables, save the water, and keep warm. Put bread rolls in oven to heat.

Finish pineapple gravy, put plates to warm.

9.00: Dish bread rolls, garnish and serve potted shrimps.

Reheat gravy before serving main course.

Menu 8

You could substitute leg or shoulder of lamb
(it would be cheaper), but this dish looks more
'partyish'!

Blue Cheese Pâté (p. 114)

* * *

Crown of Lamb or Guard of Honour (p. 73)

Apricot Stuffing (p. 73) Scalloped Potatoes (p. 85)

Roast Potatoes and Parsnips   New/Boiled Potatoes

Mangetout/Peas   Carrot Sticks   Broccoli

Gravy   Mint Sauce (p. 152)

* * *

Lemon Syllabub (p. 142)

The week before: Order crown roast or guard of honour.

Make and freeze blue cheese pâté. Make and freeze apricot stuffing. Make mint sauce, and store in fridge.

The night before: Take pâté from freezer, defrost in fridge. Take stuffing from freezer, or soak apricots to make stuffing.

On the day: Prepare pâté if not pre-frozen. Prepare stuffing if not pre-frozen.

Prepare roast, put aside in roasting tin.

Prepare scalloped potatoes. Peel or scrub roast/boiled/new potatoes and leave in cold water.

Peel parsnips, leave in cold water with a little lemon juice.

Prepare fresh vegetables and put aside.

Prepare gravy mix. Make or dish mint sauce.

Make syllabub, put in dishes and into fridge.

Slice pâté, put on plates and leave in fridge, prepare chosen garnish and bread or rolls and butter.

6.30: Heat the oven at 200°C/400°F/gas 6–7.

6.45: Put scalloped potatoes on top oven shelf.

Put extra stuffing on lower shelf.

7.15ish: Take stuffing from oven if cooked and keep warm, or put on floor of oven to finish cooking (if room, stuffing can be cooked later, going in oven at 8.00). Put roast in oven on lower shelf.

7.30: Par boil potatoes and parsnips, heat fat in roasting tin and put vegetables to roast on top shelf.

Take stuffing from oven, keep warm.

8.30: Cook boiled/new potatoes.

Cook fresh and frozen vegetables.

8.45: Check dishes in oven, lower oven heat to 100°C/200°F/gas ½–1.

Dish roast, keep warm.

Dish roast vegetables and keep warm.

Drain and dish fresh and frozen vegetables and keep warm – keep vegetable water.

Make gravy using meat juices and vegetable water.

Garnish starter.

9.00: Serve starter.

Garnish joint with paper cutlet frills and reheat gravy before serving main course.

VEGETARIAN MEALS

Menu 1

Don't mention it's 'vegetarian' and no-one will notice!

Melon with Sorbet (p. 107)

* * *

Saucy Vegetable Pancakes (p. 76)

Cheesy Potatoes   New/Boiled Potatoes

Cauliflower/Broccoli   Mangetout Peas

Green Salad with Vinaigrette Dressing (p. 101 and 154)

* * *

Gooseberry Fool with Shortbread Biscuits (p. 138)

The week before: Prepare vegetable pancakes. Freeze in sauce if making tomato pancakes, but without sauce if making avocado pancakes; make avocado sauce on the day and pour over defrosted pancakes.

Make vinaigrette dressing.

The night before: Take pancakes from freezer.

On the day: Prepare vegetable pancakes if not pre-frozen, or make avocado sauce and pour over defrosted avocado pancakes.

Make gooseberry fool, put into a dish and into fridge. Put biscuits ready.

Prepare green salad, take vinaigrette from fridge but do not mix.

Prepare cheesy potatoes, put aside. Scrub or peel new/boiled potatoes, leave in cold water.

Prepare chosen fresh vegetables.

Prepare melon, leave in fridge, ready to fill with sorbet.

8.00: Heat the oven at 200°C/400°F/gas 6–7.

8.15: Put pancakes in oven on lower shelf.

8.20: Put cheesy potatoes in oven on top shelf.
8.30: Put new/boiled potatoes on to cook.
Cook fresh and frozen vegetables.
8.45: Toss salad in dressing.
Check dishes in oven; if cooked, turn oven down to
100°C/200°F/gas ½–1.
Drain vegetables, dish and keep warm.
Drain new/boiled potatoes, dish and keep warm.
Fill melon with sorbet.
9.00: Serve starter.

Menu 2

Quite a substantial meal, absolutely delicious.

Oeufs Avocado (p. 111)

* * *

Creamy Mushroom Puffs (p. 78)

*Pommes Boulanger (p. 87) Potato/Parsnip Castles
New Potatoes   French/Runner Beans
Courgettes   Broad Beans
Mixed Green Salad (p. 101) Vinaigrette Dressing (p. 154)*

* * *

Fresh Strawberries (p. 133)/Exotic Fruit Salad (p. 135)

Cream or Crème Fraiche or Greek Yoghurt

The week before: Prepare and bake and freeze pastry
cases.
Prepare potato/parsnip castles and freeze uncooked.
Make vinaigrette, store in fridge.
The night before: If you're going to be rushed and don't
have a freezer, bake pastry cases, store in airtight tin.
Hardboil eggs, shell, store in fridge in a lidded container.

On the day: Take potato/parsnip castles from freezer.

Take pastry cases from freezer or bake cases and put aside.

Prepare mushroom filling and put aside – see recipe. Prepare pommes boulanger, put aside.

Make avocado sauce for starter.

Prepare mixed salad, put in fridge. Prepare oeufs avocado, put in fridge without sauce, until time to serve.

Prepare, dish and garnish fresh strawberries or exotic fruit salad. Dish up chosen cream, put in fridge.

Prepare fresh vegetables, put aside.

Rinse herbs for garnish, put aside.

6.30: Heat the oven at 200°C/400°F/gas 6–7.

6.45: Put pommes boulanger in oven.

8.30: Put potato/parsnip castles in oven. Cook new potatoes. Cook fresh and frozen vegetables.

8.35: Dress salad. Dress egg avocado with sauce.

Check pommes boulanger or potato/parsnip castles, put on lower oven shelf.

8.45: Put pastry cases in oven for 2–3 minutes.

Put mushroom filling and cream ready to finish.

Reduce oven heat to 100°C/200°F/gas ½–1. Dish potato/parsnip castles, keep hot. Drain and dish vegetables, keep hot.

Leave pastry cases to keep warm.

9.00: Serve starter.

When the starter is finished, get someone else to clear the plates and take in the vegetables while you heat and finish the creamy mushroom mixture, then fill the mushroom puffs and serve.

3 SIMPLY SUPER
THE MAIN COURSE RECIPES

Keep it simple, especially if you're not a very experienced cook. You're not competing with a restaurant meal. It's far better to prepare a simple menu very well than a complicated one badly – after all, most chefs probably have far more time, training, assistants and equipment than you do! The simplest of meals can be a real treat if well cooked and beautifully presented – a crispy golden dish of lasagne and a really fresh tossed green salad, or a tasty casserole served with a lovely white cauliflower, garnished with yoghurt and a shake of paprika, can be just as attractive as expensive out-of-season produce with complicated sauces that need lots of attention at the last moment.

BEEF OR VEGETABLE LASAGNE

Make meat or vegetable lasagne according to taste or budget – lentils are much cheaper than beef. Can be made in advance or frozen uncooked and defrosted before putting in the oven and timing it so that it's cooked when your guests arrive.

Preparation time: 15 mins. Cooking time: 40–50 mins.
(plus time for making Bolognese sauce).

1 quantity of Beef or Vegetable Bolognese Sauce – see pages 47/48
1 pint/600ml Cheese Sauce – see page 150
1 packet 'pre-cooked' type lasagne
2–3 tblsp grated Parmesan cheese

Prepare chosen Bolognese sauce and cheese sauce.

Allow 3–4 strips of lasagne per person according to appetite. You will need a large, ovenproof dish, approximately 10"/25cm square by 2–3"/5–7cm deep; buy a foil dish if necessary – it saves washing up – or use two smaller dishes. The two sauces must be quite runny, as the lasagne will absorb liquid during cooking, so, if necessary, stir ½–1 cup extra milk into the cheese sauce, to make runny, pouring sauces.

Heat the oven at 180°C/350°F/gas 4–5.

Put a layer of Bolognese sauce into the dish, cover with a single layer of lasagne strips, and top with a little cheese sauce. Repeat layers until all the ingredients are used up, ending with a thick layer of cheese sauce (be sure to reserve enough for this top layer). Sprinkle with Parmesan and bake in the hot oven for 40–50 minutes (according to the size of the dish) until the top is a golden brown. The

uncooked dish can be frozen, then defrosted overnight
and cooked as above.

Serve with hot bread rolls or French bread (popped in
the oven for the last 5 minutes of cooking time) and a
mixed green salad.

LENTIL BOLOGNESE SAUCE

Useful if you have a vegetarian guest, and quite acceptable to "non veges" when used in lasagne. Use canned or
dried lentils, according to the time available (canned
lentils are ready cooked, dried lentils need cooking
beforehand), or make sauce in advance and freeze to
defrost overnight when required.

Preparation and cooking time: 30 mins.
  plus 45 mins. for dried green lentils
  or plus 20 mins. for dried red lentils

8 oz/250g dried green or red lentils (weight before cooking
  or 2 × 14 oz/397g cans cooked lentils
2–3 onions
1–2 cloves garlic or ½ tsp garlic powder
2–3 sticks celery
2–3 carrots
2 tblsp oil for frying
2 large cans (14 oz/397g) tomatoes or 1 lb/½kg fresh ones
2 tblsp tomato purée or ketchup
1 dried tomato in oil (optional from Italian shops)
Salt, pepper, 1 tsp sugar
2 tsp mixed herbs, ½ tsp Worcester sauce
½–1 pint/300–600ml liquid (save lentil water from cooked
  lentils or use liquid from canned lentils)

Rinse dried lentils and cook in boiling water, without salt, for 45 minutes (green lentils) or 20 minutes (red lentils). Drain, saving the water for the sauce.

Peel and chop onions and garlic cloves, wash and chop celery, peel and grate or chop carrots. Heat oil in a large saucepan over a moderate heat and fry onion, garlic and celery gently until soft, about 4–5 minutes. Add carrot, pre-cooked or canned lentils, canned tomatoes or chopped tomatoes and juice, tomato purée or ketchup, chopped dried tomato (if used), and stir well, adding enough of the chosen liquid to make a runny sauce. Season with salt, pepper, sugar, herbs and Worcester sauce, and bring to the boil, stirring occasionally. Lower heat and simmer for 15–20 minutes, adding extra liquid if it seems too stiff, to produce a thick, tasty sauce.

Note: if using the sauce for lasagne (see page 46), add a little more liquid to make a runny sauce, as the dry lasagne absorbs the extra liquid while cooking.

TRADITIONAL BEEF BOLOGNESE SAUCE

A spicy meat sauce, delicious with all kinds of pasta. Can be made in advance and frozen, defrosting before use. Remember to take the Bolognese from the freezer the night before. The recipe uses 1¼ lb/½kg minced meat, which is convenient for lasagne, but for other meals, such as chilli or spaghetti, you will need to make double the recipe to feed six people.

Preparation and cooking time: 1¼–1½ hours.

2–3 onions
1–2 cloves garlic or ½ tsp garlic powder
2 carrots

1–2 rashers bacon
1–2 tblsp oil for frying
1¼ lb/½kg good quality minced beef
1 large can (14 oz/397g) tomatoes or 1 lb/½kg fresh ones
2 tblsp tomato purée or ketchup
1 dried tomato in oil (optional, from Italian shops)
1 beef stock cube and ¾ pint/½ litre hot water
Salt, pepper, 1 tsp sugar
2 tsp mixed herbs, ½ tsp Worcester sauce

Peel and finely chop onions and fresh garlic. Peel and grate carrots, chop bacon. Heat oil in a large saucepan or casserole and fry onion, garlic and bacon over a moderate heat for 4–5 minutes. Add minced beef and continue cooking, stirring continually, for a further 5 minutes until meat is lightly browned. Add canned tomatoes or washed, chopped fresh ones, tomato purée, finely chopped dried tomato if used, carrot, crumbled stock cube and hot water, stirring well. Season with salt and pepper, stir in sugar, mixed herbs and a dash of Worcester sauce. Bring to the boil, then lower heat and simmer over a very low heat, stirring occasionally, for 45–60 minutes, until meat is tender, and the sauce is nice and thick.

CHILLI CON CARNE

Make as hot as you like and serve poured over jacket potatoes with a fresh green salad to cool the palate.

Preparation and cooking time: 1½ hours or 15 mins. if using pre-prepared Bolognese sauce.

2 quantities Beef Bolognese sauce
1–2 tsp hot chilli powder – or according to taste
½–1 tsp hot Tabasco sauce – or according to taste
2 large (15 oz/430g) cans cooked kidney beans

Prepare Bolognese sauce – see page 48 – adding chilli powder and tabasco with the other seasonings. Add drained cooked kidney beans and simmer in the sauce for the last 15 minutes of the cooking time. Taste and adjust seasoning. Put aside until needed or freeze and defrost when required. Reheat chilli over a low heat if necessary, simmering gently for a few minutes to make sure it's really hot before serving.

To serve: Bake jacket potatoes, see page 84, timing them to be ready and keeping warm in the oven while you are serving the first course. Serve with butter and/or a cold yoghurt and cucumber sauce (see page 153) and a green salad prepared in advance.

VEGETABLE CHILLI

Prepare and serve as for Chilli Con Carne, using the recipe for Lentil Bolognese on page 47.

NORWEGIAN SPECIAL

Fresh whole prawns with garlic bread and salad.

This makes a really different and easy summer dinner party, but you must use whole prawns in the shells (available at fishmongers or the fresh fish counter at the supermarket) as peeled frozen prawns aren't quite the same. Serve a pre-prepared hot or cold soup as a starter, if you wish, or just serve a cold sweet and cheese, and you have a lovely meal with very little to do at the last minute, apart from heating the garlic bread and tossing the salad.

Preparation time: Prawns – 5 mins.
    Garlic Bread – 10 mins. plus 5 mins. heating time.

Salad – 10–15 mins.
Vinaigrette – 5 mins.

Allow ¾ lb/⅓kg fresh prawns per person (weighed in shells) so for 6 people buy **4½ lb/2kg whole prawns, one 16 oz/450g jar mayonnaise and 2–3 tblsp plain yoghurt or double cream (optional)**
or 1 quantity avocado sauce, see page 154
1–2 lemons, cut into wedges for garnish

Rinse prawns in a colander under cold running water, drain well. Divide the prawns between 6 large glasses or beer mugs, topping each glass with one or two of the largest prawns. Store in the fridge.

Mix mayonnaise with yoghurt or cream (if used) and pile into a serving bowl, or make avocado cream (see page 154), keeping the sauce quite thick, and store in fridge.

Prepare garlic bread (see page 146), put aside until time to heat, just before you want to eat. Prepare salad and vinaigrette dressing (see page 154).

Provide guests with dinner plates for their peeled prawns and salad, side plates for the garlic bread, empty dishes for prawn shells, and, if you've got enough dishes, finger bowls of warm water as it's a sticky business peeling prawns. Also you'll need plenty of paper napkins, and don't be fooled, this meal is a lot more filling than it may appear.

TOMATO BRAISED STEAK

A tasty main course, quick and easy to prepare, although it needs a long cooking time. Prepare in advance and put in fridge, or freeze and defrost overnight to be ready to cook and serve when your guests arrive, or cook in advance and reheat thoroughly just before dinner.

Preparation time: 15–20 mins.
Cooking time: 2–2½ hours.
Reheating time: 20–30 mins.

3–4 onions
2–3 tblsp cooking oil
6 slices braising steak, each slice approx. 6 oz/150g
  (about 2¼ lb/1kg beef)
1 large can (14 oz/394g) tomatoes or 1 lb/450g fresh ones
1 beef stock cube and ¾ pint/450ml hot water
1 tblsp cornflour or flour
1 tsp gravy powder
2 tblsp tomato purée or tomato sauce
Salt, pepper, 1 tsp sugar
1 tsp mixed herbs
Dash Worcester sauce and/or Soy sauce
Handful fresh parsley (optional)

Heat the oven at 170°C/325°F/gas 3–4. Peel and slice
onions, heat oil in a large frying pan over a moderate heat,
and fry braising steak slices for a few minutes on each side
(cut slices in half if they are very long and trim off any
gristle or lumps of fat), to brown the meat and seal in the
juices. Put meat into a large ovenproof dish or casserole –
a wide dish is best so that meat is in only one or two layers.

Put onion slices into frying pan, adding a little more oil
if needed, and fry gently for 4–5 minutes until soft, stir in
tinned or washed, sliced tomatoes and pour over the
meat. Dissolve stock cube in hot water. Mix flour or
cornflour and gravy powder to a smooth paste with a little
cold water, then stir the stock into the paste to make a
smooth gravy. Stir in tomato purée or sauce, salt, pepper,
sugar, herbs and sauces and pour over meat, making sure
meat is well covered with sauce or it will dry up – stir in a
little more water if necessary. Cover with a lid or piece of

foil and cook in the moderate oven for about 2–2½ hours, until meat is tender, stirring occasionally.

Carefully taste the gravy (don't burn your tongue) and adjust seasoning if necessary. Sprinkle with washed, snipped parsley and serve, or keep hot until needed.

If reheating casserole from cold before dinner, allow approx 30 minutes in a *hot* oven *(200°C/400°F/gas 6–7)* and make sure the meal is heated right through, not just warmed, before serving. Serve with jacket potatoes or a potato dish that can be cooked in the oven above the casserole, timed to be ready when you want to eat, and a quickly cooked fresh or frozen green vegetable.

PORK IN CIDER SAUCE

A rich, savoury casserole, which smells marvellous when cooking. Prepare in advance and cook in the oven, timed to be ready when you want to eat. Cook a potato dish in the oven at the same time, and a green vegetable.

Preparation time: 20 mins.   *Cooking time: 1¼ hours.*

6 pork steaks
1 tblsp cooking oil
2–3 large onions
2 large cooking apples
1 chicken stock cube
½–¾ pint/300–450ml cider or cider and water
2 tsp mixed herbs, salt and pepper
2–3 tblsp double cream, plain yoghurt or soured cream
Handful fresh parsley

Heat the oven at 180°C/350°F/gas 4–5. Trim any excess fat from steaks and cut each steak in half. Heat oil in a large frying pan over a moderate heat and fry meat on both sides for a few minutes until browned. Put into a casserole. Peel and slice onions, peel core and chop apples and fry together in the frying pan for 4–5 minutes until the onion is soft. Add to casserole. Crumble stock cube into frying pan and add ½ pint/300ml cider, stirring well to collect all the juices from the pan, then pour sauce over the meat, adding more cider/water so that it just covers the meat. Season with herbs, salt and pepper. Cover with a lid and bake in the moderate oven for 50–60 minutes until meat is tender, or freeze, or put in fridge until time to cook.

To serve: Swirl the cream or yoghurt into the hot casserole and sprinkle a little washed snipped parsley on the top.

GOULASH

Traditionally cooked on top of the stove (or over the fire in a big iron pot), but it's much easier to pop it into a slow oven, timed to be ready to eat when your guests arrive. Serve with plain noodles (not too many as there are potatoes already in the goulash) and a plain green vegetable or salad to complement the rich, spicy sauce.

Preparation time: 20 mins.   *Cooking time: 2–2½ hours.*

4 large onions
2¼ lb/1kg stewing beef
2 tblsp cooking oil
1–2 tblsp *paprika* pepper (not cayenne pepper)
1 glass red wine
1 large (14 oz/397g) can tomatoes
2–3 tblsp tomato purée or ketchup
1 beef stock cube and ½ pint/300ml hot water
Salt, pepper, 1 tsp mixed herbs

1 tsp sugar
1 lb/½kg potatoes
6 oz/150g mushrooms
¼ pint/150g carton soured cream or plain yoghurt
Handful fresh parsley

Heat the oven at 170°C/325°F/gas 3–4. Peel and slice onions, trim and cube beef (1″/2½cm cubes). Heat oil in a casserole or large saucepan over a moderate heat and fry onions for 4–5 minutes until soft. Add cubed beef and continue frying for a further 4–5 minutes until beef is browned on all sides. Sprinkle in paprika and stir over the heat, adding wine. Mix in tomatoes and tomato purée or ketchup, dissolve stock cube in ½ pint/300ml hot water and pour over meat mixture. Season with salt, pepper, herbs and sugar, stir well and transfer casserole into the moderate oven, or turn down heat on stove to very low and simmer goulash in casserole or saucepan for 1–1¼ hours. Stir occasionally.

Peel potatoes, cut into large bite-sized chunks and add to goulash, continue cooking for a further hour. Wash and slice large mushrooms, leave button mushrooms whole, and add to goulash for last 15 minutes of cooking time.

To serve: Stir in soured cream or yoghurt, sprinkle with washed, snipped parsley and a further shake of paprika.

The goulash can be made in advance and put in the fridge, or frozen and defrosted overnight, then heated through in the moderate oven or over a very gentle heat on top of the stove for 30–40 minutes before serving; make sure the meat is completely cooked, not just warmed. Cook the noodles and green vegetables at the last minute and keep warm while serving the starter.

CHEATING CANNELLONI

This is an idea for what to serve when you've been out all day, have made no preparations, and have people coming to dinner that evening. It's a bit expensive, but cheaper and more imaginative than sending out for a pizza or taking everyone to the local Chinese restaurant! Serve the cannelloni with a crisp green salad and bread rolls or garlic bread; you can buy pre-packs of salad if necessary, and frozen garlic bread, all ready to heat in the oven.

Preparation time: 5 mins.   Cooking time: 30 mins.

12 fresh cannelloni (buy from the fresh pasta shop), stuffed with beef, ricotta and nuts, etc. Allow 2 cannelloni each for average appetites, but you know your friends better than I do!
2 pints/1200ml fresh or frozen tomato sauce (homemade if you have it, or buy a sauce from the pasta shop)
3–4 tblsp grated Parmesan cheese

Heat the oven at 180°C/350°F/gas 4–5. Put cannelloni in one layer into one large or two smaller ovenproof dishes (keep meat and vegetarian stuffings separate so that you can offer a choice if you've bought both), and pour sauce over the top to cover the cannelloni. Sprinkle with grated Parmesan cheese. Cover lightly with foil and put in the fridge until needed, then bake in the hot oven for 25–30 minutes, removing the foil for the last 10 minutes, to brown the cheesy topping. Time it so that it's ready when you want to eat. Any extra sauce can be heated gently in a saucepan just before serving, poured into a jug and served separately.

Put the garlic bread into the oven for the last 10 minutes of cooking time (or according to instructions on the packet), or warm the fresh bread rolls in the oven for 3–4 minutes. Assemble green salad, cover with cling film and keep cool until needed. Make a vinaigrette dressing (see page 154) or buy a bottle of dressing from the supermarket – do not add the dressing until the last minute or the salad will go limp.

Serve the main course accompanied by plenty of Italian red wine and enjoy a pleasant evening.

4 POSHER NOSH
THE MAIN COURSE RECIPES

Now show off your skills, as these recipes are a little more extravagant, and you can make them more showy if you wish by adding extra choice of vegetables or perhaps offering several desserts. Presentation makes all the difference, so garnish and decorate lavishly but tastefully, complement the food with an attractive table setting, and keep to the 'simple but perfect' approach, and your meals will be impressive.

PORK AND BEANSPROUT CASSEROLE

A casserole with a most intriguing flavour. Although it

looks time-consuming, most of the preparation time involves leaving the meat in the marinade – do this overnight or prepare the rest of the meal while you're waiting. I use pork steaks, but any lean boned pork is suitable. There are so many vegetables in the casserole already that noodles or plain potatoes and a plain green vegetable if you wish, are sufficient accompaniment. Prepare in advance and cook. Store in fridge or freeze and defrost overnight to reheat just before your guests arrive.

Preparation time: 25 mins. plus 1–2 hours or overnight marinating time.
Cooking time: 1¼ hours or ¾ hour cooking plus ¾ hour reheating.

Marinade: **2 tblsp vegetable oil**
2 tblsp sugar, white or brown
2 tblsp wine, sherry or cider
3 tblsp vinegar
1 tblsp Worcester sauce
1 tblsp Soy sauce
1 tsp mixed herbs
Salt, pepper

2¼ lb/1kg lean boned pork – steaks, boned leg or shoulder
3 onions
3–4 sticks celery
4 oz/100g mushrooms
1 small green and 1 small red pepper
4 tblsp vegetable oil
1 chicken stock cube and 1 pint/600ml hot water
1 tblsp cornflour
1 can – 15 oz/420g – pineapple chunks, in juice or syrup
1 carton fresh beansprouts or 1 can 9 oz/250g beansprouts
  (the fresh ones are nicest)

Measure all marinade ingredients into a large bowl or dish and mix well. Trim pork, cut into 1″/2½cm cubes and stir them into the marinade, making sure all the meat is covered by the liquid. Leave to absorb the flavours for at least 1–2 hours (it can be left over night in the fridge), stirring occasionally. Peel and thinly slice onions, wash and cut celery into 1″/2½cm lengths, wash and slice large mushrooms (leave small mushrooms whole), wash, de-seed and slice peppers into 2″/5cm strips.

Heat the oven at 170°C/325°F/gas 3–4. Heat 2 tblsp oil in a large frying pan over a moderate heat, remove pork from marinade (use a slotted spoon, and keep the marinade), and fry pork in the oil for a few minutes, until brown on all sides. Put pork into a large casserole dish. Add a little more oil to the frying pan and fry onions and celery for 4–5 minutes until soft, then add peppers and mushrooms and fry for a few more minutes until just soft, then add to pork.

Dissolve stock cube in the hot water, pour into frying pan and stir round to scrape up all the juices. Pour into the casserole. Put cornflour into a small basin, drain pine-apple cubes and put aside, mix a little pineapple juice with the cornflour to make a smooth, runny paste, then stir in rest of pineapple juice and stir all the liquid into the casserole and mix well. Cover with a lid or piece of cooking foil and cook in the moderate oven for about ¾ hour, stirring occasionally.

The casserole can now be cooled and put into the fridge, or frozen to defrost when needed.

To finish casserole: stir in pineapple cubes and washed drained fresh or drained canned beansprouts. Replace lid and cook or reheat for a further 20–30 minutes, until meat and veg are all cooked and the sauce is thick and tasty. Adjust seasoning with salt and pepper.

Serve with plain noodles, cooked while the casserole is finishing, or jacket potatoes cooked in the oven with the

casserole (see page 84) and a quickly cooked green
vegetable; broccoli or French beans are nice, but with so
many veg already in the casserole you won't need many
accompaniments.

CHICKEN IN CRUNCHY PEANUT SAUCE WITH SWEETCORN

The peanut butter in which the chicken is cooked gives a
nice crunch to contrast with the chicken, quite a change
from the more usual type of chicken casseroles. Prepare
the casserole in advance and cook in the oven, timed to be
ready when you want to eat. Serve with Ki's Special
Potatoes (page 88) cooked in the oven with the chicken
and a plain green vegetable or a green salad. Use chicken
joints or boneless chicken breasts for this dish (but not a
mixture!).

Preparation time: 20 mins.
Cooking time: 30–40 mins. for boneless chicken breast
  1–1¼ hours for chicken joints
  (longest time if cooking from cold).

2 large onions
1 clove garlic or ¼ tsp garlic granules
1 tblsp vegetable oil
2 tblsp crunchy peanut butter
6 chicken breast joints – on the bone or boneless
2 chicken stock cubes
¾ pint/450ml hot water
¼ pint/150ml milk
2–3 tblsp salted peanuts and/or 2-3 tblsp chopped walnuts
1 large 12 oz/330g can sweetcorn
Handful fresh chives or parsley

Heat the oven at 180°C/350°F/gas 4–5. Peel and finely chop onions and garlic. Heat oil and 1 tblsp peanut butter in a frying pan over a moderate heat, and fry chicken pieces gently for 4–5 minutes until browned on both sides, and place in a casserole or ovenproof dish. Put onion and garlic into the pan and continue to fry for 3–5 minutes until softened but not browned; spoon it over the chicken. Dissolve chicken stock cubes in hot water, put in the frying pan and scrape up all the juices. Stir in milk and remaining spoonful of peanut butter, peanuts and/or chopped walnuts. Pour sauce over chicken and cover with a piece of foil.

Put aside in fridge until ready to cook, then bake in the oven, timed to be ready when you want to serve the meal, stirring in drained sweetcorn for last 10 minutes of cooking time. Garnish with washed, snipped chives or parsley and serve piping hot.

HERB STUFFED FISH STEAKS

First of all make sure all your guests like fish, or you've got problems at dinner time! Fish prices vary greatly according to the weather, time of year etc., so choose whatever looks fresh and is good value – cod, halibut, tuna or even turbot steaks. Cod is usually the cheapest, but sometimes there are special offers available for the more exotic fish. The sharp lemon stuffing gives the fish a nice flavour. Prepare steaks in advance and bake them, timed to be ready when you want to serve the meal. Serve with tomato scalloped potatoes which will cook in the oven with the fish, or potato castles prepared in advance and heated in the oven at the last minute, and a green vegetable for colour.

Preparation time: 20 mins.   *Cooking time: 25–35 mins.*

Stuffing: **1 small onion**
1 lemon
1 packet/4 oz/100g thyme and parsley stuffing mix
Handful fresh parsley
1 tsp mixed herbs
Salt, pepper
6 fish steaks – cod, halibut, tuna, turbot, etc.
2 oz/50g butter
2 lemons for garnish

Heat the oven at 180°C/375°F/gas 5–6. Make stuffing – peel and finely chop onion, put into a small pan with ½ cup water and 1 tblsp lemon juice. Bring to the boil and simmer for 4–5 minutes, until onion is soft. Remove from heat, stir in stuffing mix, grated lemon rind, washed snipped parsley, herbs, salt and pepper, and mix to a stiff paste with lemon juice. Leave to thicken for 5 minutes.

Wash and trim fish steaks and arrange in a *very well buttered* wide, shallow ovenproof dish, big enough to hold all the steaks in one layer – or use two dishes. Put a large spoonful of stuffing in the centre of each steak, heaping it up slightly. Dot fish and stuffing with flakes of butter and cover lightly with a well greased foil lid. Put in the fridge until needed.

Bake in the hot oven for 25–35 minutes, timing fish to be cooked when you want to eat the main course. You will need a fish slice to slide each steak with its stuffing carefully onto the plates. Garnish with big lemon wedges.

ROAST PORK – TRADITIONAL SUNDAY LUNCH OR DINNER 🔥

What could be nicer on a lazy Sunday than a hot roast dinner with all the trimmings? It's equally good any other day of the week too! Pork is one of the more economical roasts, sold with the bone in (supposedly more flavoursome), or boned and rolled (easier to carve). Leg of pork is leaner and more expensive than shoulder, but either makes an excellent meal.

Pork roasting joints:
Leg – the prime roasting joint, leanest, most expensive, often sold with the bone in.
Loin – chops, left in one piece, not cut up.
Shoulder – cheaper but more fat, usually sold boned and rolled.

Allow approx. 8 oz/225g per serving (6 oz/175g boned and rolled), so a joint weighing 3–4 lb/1½–2kg should serve 6 people – unless you want cold meat left for tomorrow or everyone has very large appetites! Pork is traditionally served with sage and onion stuffing and apple sauce, roast and/or boiled potatoes and fresh root and green vegetables and thick gravy.

Check the weight of the joint when you buy it, as cooking time depends on the weight. Allow 25 mins. per lb/450g plus 25 mins. extra i.e. a 4 lb/1.8kg joint will take approx. 2–2¼ hours.

Heat oven at 200°C/400°F/gas 6–7. Rub pork skin with a little oil and sprinkle with salt to make the crackling really crisp and give it a good flavour. Place joint in the roasting tin with just a little oil or fat to stop it sticking, and put tin into the hot oven. Calculate cooking time to be ready to dish up 15 minutes before you want to eat. After 20–30 minutes, when the crackling has crisped, cover the joint, or the whole tin, lightly with foil, to stop the meat getting too brown.

Roast Potatoes, Roast Parsnips, Roast Onions – cook round the meat for the last hour of cooking time, or cook in a separate roasting tin above the meat, pages 83, 96, 95.

Stuffing – prepare in advance and cook separately in a well greased ovenproof dish on the shelf above the meat – you may have to do a bit of juggling around to fit in with the potatoes, but stuffing can be cooked first and kept warm if necessary – see page 147.

Apple Sauce – make in advance – see page 152. Store in fridge and serve cold or reheat gently in a saucepan or on the floor of the oven for 10–15 minutes.

Boiled/New Potatoes – see page 82/3. Prepare and cook, timed to be ready with the meat. Drain cooked potatoes (save the veg water for the gravy) and keep warm.

Root Veg. – carrots or swede (see pages 94, 96) give a nice splash of colour to the meal. Prepare and cook to be ready with the meat.

Green Veg. – fresh or frozen – cabbage, sprouts, cauli, peas, runner or French beans, according to season and taste. Prepare in advance and cook to be ready just before you want to eat – see pages 94–97.

Potato and Vegetable dishes cooked in the oven – e.g. scalloped potatoes, spicy red cabbage. Serving these kinds of dishes saves a lot of last-minute panic, as they can be prepared in advance and cooked in the oven with the meat, timed to be ready when you want to eat.

To serve: Test that the meat is cooked by prodding the joint with a fork or knife. If juices are clear, the meat is cooked; if pink, cook for a bit longer (pork should *never* be served underdone, as it can cause food poisoning): the meat should be pale-coloured not pink. Lift joint onto a hot serving plate, leave to rest before carving, while you dish up the veg and make the gravy.

Gravy: Prepare gravy mix in advance – see page 149 –

using a little more cornflour to make a thick gravy, and pouring in the juices from the roasting tin. Use the reserved potato or vegetable water to make a smooth brown gravy, and cook until gravy thickens.

STEAK AND KIDNEY PIE

Just watch the eyes of your male guests light up when you put this dish on the table! Can be prepared in advance or frozen and defrosted overnight ready to cook, timed to be ready when your guests arrive. Serve roast potatoes and a vegetable dish (spicy red cabbage is good) that can cook in the oven with the pie, or new or boiled potatoes and a quickly cooked green vegetable – a lovely white cauli and the ubiquitous frozen peas look and taste good.

Preparation and cooking time: 2–2½ hours (pie filling).
Cooking time: 25–30 mins. (finished pie with crust).

2–3 large onions
2¼ lb/1kg stewing steak
8 oz/200g ox kidney
3–4 carrots
2 tblsp vegetable oil
1 glass red wine (optional)
1 beef stock cube and ¾ pint/450ml water
1 tsp mixed herbs
6 oz/150g mushrooms
1 packet frozen or chilled puff pastry and milk for brushing

Peel and chop onions. Trim steak and cut into 1"/2½cm cubes, trim and cut kidney into smaller cubes. Peel and slice carrots into ½"/1cm rings. Heat oil in a large saucepan or casserole over a moderate heat and fry gently for 4–5 minutes until soft. Add steak and kidney and continue frying for a further 5 minutes, until meat is browned and sealed on all sides. Add carrots and wine (if used). Dissolve stock cube in *½ pint/300ml* hot water and pour over meat, add extra water if necessary just to cover meat completely. Stir in herbs and bring to the boil, then reduce heat and simmer over a low heat or in a low oven (170°C/325°F/gas 3–4) for 1¾–2 hours until meat is tender, adding washed sliced mushrooms for last 15 minutes of cooking time.

Defrost pastry.

Spoon cooked meat mixture into a large pie dish or two smaller ones, large enough to give everyone a good-sized piece of crust, approximately 2½–3 pint/1½ litre dish, and reserve most of the meat gravy. Season with salt and pepper.

Roll out pastry slightly larger than the pie dish, approximately ¼"/½cm thick (or divide in two and roll out each piece to fit two dishes), lift pastry over the rolling pin and lay it over the pie. Ease gently into shape and trim edges with a knife. Knock up edges. Roll out trimmings, cut into leaves and use to decorate the top of the pie. Brush crust with a little milk and make a tiny hole in the middle of the crust. Put in fridge or freeze and defrost when ready to bake.

Heat the oven at 200°C/400°F/gas 6–7, or as instructed on pastry packet. Bake pie in the hot oven for 20–30 minutes according to size, until crust is well risen, crisp and golden – turn pie during cooking if necessary.

Make *steak and kidney gravy:*

1 tblsp cornflour
2 tsp gravy powder
1 wine-glass red wine or cold water
Gravy left from cooking the meat

Mix cornflour and gravy powder to a smooth paste with wine or water, and stir in reserved meat gravy. Pour gravy into a saucepan, bring to the boil, stirring all the time until gravy thickens. Pour into a jug and serve with the pie.

The pie can be timed to be cooked when your guests arrive, and kept warm in a very low oven (100°C/200°F/gas ½–1) until you are ready to serve the meal.

POT ROAST BEEF IN VEGETABLE GRAVY

A different, very tasty roast dinner. The vegetables and gravy are cooked round the meat, so everything is ready to eat when the meat is cooked. Serve with roast or jacket potatoes or a potato dish cooked in the oven above the meat – scalloped potatoes are easy – and a quickly cooked green vegetable, and/or a green salad for a delicious meal. If you feel ambitious, you can serve Yorkshire puds too, but these are definitely last-minute extras for the experienced, brave or foolish cook!

Preparation time: 20 mins.
Cooking time: 1–1½ hours. Allow 15–20 mins per lb/500g and 15–20 mins. extra, depending how rare you like beef.

3–3½ lb/1½kg joint beef – topside, top rump or silverside
2–3 medium onions
2–3 rashers bacon
3–4 large carrots
1 small swede
3–4 sticks celery
3 tblsp vegetable oil
1 wine-glass red wine or sherry – optional but nice
2 beef stock cubes
1 pint/600ml hot water, approx.
2 tsp mixed herbs

Salt, pepper
To thicken gravy: **1 tblsp cornflour**
2 tsp gravy browning
Red wine, sherry or water to mix

If you don't have a really large frying pan, use a wok or saucepan big enough to hold all the vegetables.

Rinse joint and dry with kitchen paper. Peel and slice onions. Derind and chop bacon. Peel carrots and cut into ½"/1cm rings. Peel swede thickly and cut into ¾"/2cm cubes. Trim celery, cut into 1"/2cm lengths. Heat oil in a large frying pan over a moderate heat and fry onion and bacon for 4–5 minutes until soft, but not brown. Add carrots, swede and celery and continue frying for a further 5–6 minutes, stirring continuously to absorb the fat. Stir in booze if used, dissolve stock cubes in ¾ *pint/450ml* hot water, stir in herbs and bring to the boil.

Remove from heat, and carefully ladle vegetable mixture into a large roasting tin, pouring in all the gravy from the pan – there should be enough liquid just to cover the veg, if not stir in a little more water. Place beef on top of veg, cover tin completely with cooking foil, and put aside until time to cook, calculating it so that the beef is ready just before your guests arrive.

To cook: Heat the oven at 200°C/400°F/gas 6–7. Carefully (remember the tin is full and heavy) put roasting tin into the hot oven and roast for the calculated time, removing foil for last 20–25 minutes of cooking time to brown the beef. If making Yorkshire puds, put them into the oven to cook on the top shelf when you remove the foil from the beef. Roast potatoes can cook in a separate tin above the beef, or jacket potatoes can cook on the lower shelf – see pages 83 and 84.

To serve: Put beef onto a hot carving dish, cover with the foil and leave to stand and relax while you dish the veg.

Thicken gravy: Mix cornflour and gravy powder to a smooth, runny paste with the booze or water and stir into the hot vegetable mixture. Stir well, and either bring back to the boil over a moderate heat on top of the stove, or put the tin back in the oven and reheat for 5–10 minutes, stirring occasionally, until gravy thickens slightly – this should not be a very thick gravy, but use more cornflour if you want it to be really thick. Pour veg and gravy carefully into a large sauceboat with a ladle, or a serving bowl, and serve separately, or ladle some veg and gravy over each serving of beef.

Dish up roast or jacket potatoes, Yorkshire puds and green vegetables, and keep hot in the low oven while eating the starter (the meat will keep hot out of the oven; it may overcook if put back in the heat).

YORKSHIRE PUDDINGS

Make individual Yorkshire puds in patty or bun tins. Allow 1 or 2 puds per person – this recipe will make 6 very large or 12 smaller individual puds. Make batter in advance and store in fridge until calculated time to cook.

Preparation time: 5 mins.   Cooking time: 20–25 mins.

4 oz/100g/4 heaped tblsp plain flour
Large pinch salt
1 egg
½ pint/300ml milk
2 tblsp oil for cooking

Put flour and salt into a basin. Add egg and beat into the flour, gradually adding milk, and beating well to make a smooth batter – use a wooden spoon or mixer. Put in fridge until needed.

To cook: Heat the oven at 200°C/400°F/gas 6–7. When

oven is hot, put a little oil in each tin and heat tin on top shelf of oven for 2–3 minutes. Give batter a final stir and *pour into the hot tins*. Bake in the hot oven for 20–25 minutes, until risen, firm and golden brown (the larger puds take the longer time). Do not open oven door for the first 10–15 minutes of cooking time or puds may collapse. Place on a hot serving dish, do not cover, and serve as soon as possible, but they will keep happily while you eat the first course.

STICKY ROAST GAMMON WITH PINEAPPLE

Quite an expensive meal, but nice for a special occasion. Can be partly cooked in advance, ready to finish off in the oven just before your guests arrive. Serve with jacket potatoes cooked in the oven with the joint, or new potatoes cooked at the last minute. A vegetable dish could be cooked in the oven at the same time (mushrooms à la Grecque is nice) and served with a quickly cooked fresh or frozen green vegetable.

Buy a gammon joint from the butcher or a pre-pack from the supermarket. Allow 6–8 oz/150–250g per serving, so a joint weighing 3–3½ lb/1½–1¾kg should serve 6 people – check the weight when you buy in order to calculate the cooking time.

Gammon usually needs soaking before cooking to remove the salt. Soak smoked gammon for 3–4 hours, green (unsmoked) gammon for 1–2 hours, in a large pan of cold water.

Cooking time: allow 20 minutes per lb/450g and 20 mins. over, i.e. approx 1½ hours in total.

Heat the oven at 200°C/400°F/gas 6–7. Dry gammon on kitchen paper, wrap whole joint in a large piece of foil put it in a roasting tin and cook in the hot oven for two thirds of the calculated cooking time (approximately hour). There is no need to grease the foil, the joint wil keep moist.

While gammon is cooking, make the glaze:

3 oz/75g butter
2 oz/50g soft brown sugar
1 tsp made mustard
½–1 tsp vinegar

Cream butter and sugar until soft, beat in mustard and moisten with vinegar to make a soft paste. Remove join from oven after approximately 1 hour, and when coo enough to handle remove skin from gammon, score fa into a diamond pattern and coat with glaze, spreading the paste on thickly. The joint can now be put into a lightly greased roasting tin and put aside until time to finish.

When ready to cook, put joint into the hot oven and roast, uncovered, for approximately a further 30 minutes (the last third of the cooking time), basting occasionally with the glaze in the tin, until the meat is sticky and ligh brown.

Pineapple: Use a large 15 oz/420g can of pineapple ring in syrup or natural juice, according to taste. Make sure there's at least one ring for everyone. Slip pineapple ring into the tin with the gammon for the last 5–10 minutes o cooking time, or serve cold. Save the juice for the gravy.

To serve: Dish joint onto a hot serving plate and pile pineapple rings round. Keep warm until needed.

Gravy: Prepare gravy mix, see page 149, using the juices from the meat tin and the pineapple juice, instead of water, adding a little extra water if needed.

GUARD OF HONOUR OR CROWN ROAST WITH APRICOT STUFFING 🔥

A little more special than plain roast lamb. Prepare in advance and put into the oven so that it's timed to be ready just before you want to eat. Serve with roast potatoes, parsnips and onions in winter, all cooked in the oven with the lamb, just leaving a green vegetable and the gravy to finish at the last minute, or with new potatoes and mangetout peas in the summer. You may or may not like mint sauce or mint jelly with the apricot stuffing.

Preparation time: 30 mins. plus 2–3 hours soaking time.
Cooking time: 1–1½ hours depending on how you like the lamb – very rare or quite well done.

2 best ends of lamb (allow 2 chops per serving), now available ready prepared as Guard of Honour or Crown Roast in many supermarkets, or, ask your *very kind* butcher if he would prepare it for you – but do give him a few days' notice and a sweet smile to get him used to the idea!

Little oil for roasting
Stuffing: **3 oz/75g dried apricots**
       1 onion
       2 sticks celery
       2 thick slices bread, white or brown
       1 tblsp vegetable oil
       1 tsp mixed herbs
       1 egg
       Salt, pepper, handful fresh parsley
1 oz/25g butter

Put apricots into a basin, cover with boiling water and leave for at least 2–3 hours until soft. Drain and chop. Peel and finely chop onion. Trim and finely chop celery. Make breadcrumbs – use a blender or grater. Heat oil in a saucepan over a moderate heat, and fry onion and celery until soft, for about 4–5 minutes. Remove from heat, stir in apricots, breadcrumbs and herbs. Beat egg with a fork and add enough beaten egg to bind stuffing into a soft consistency. Season with salt and pepper and a little washed, snipped parsley. The stuffing can be made in advance or frozen and defrosted overnight before use.

To cook: Heat the oven at 200°C/400°F/gas 6–7. Put a little oil in the roasting tin or a large ovenproof dish. Stand the Guard of Honour on a thick bed of stuffing or fill the centre of the Crown Roast with stuffing, dot with butter and cover lightly with foil, any extra stuffing can be cooked in a well greased ovenproof dish and served separately – it will take 30–40 minutes to cook.

 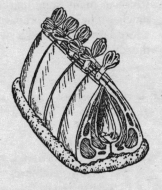

Fig. 1

(a) Crown Roast   **(b) Guard of Honour**

Put roast in the oven, calculating the cooking time so that it's ready just before you want to eat, and roast for 1–1½ hours according to taste; remove foil for last 20 minutes of the cooking time to brown the meat. Roast potatoes, parsnips and onions in a separate tin above the joint, see pages 83, 96, 95.

To serve: Very carefully slide joint and stuffing onto a hot serving plate (you will need a fish slice for this operation) or serve on the ovenproof roasting dish (which is probably much easier!). Keep warm until ready to serve. You can decorate the tips of the chops with cutlet frills if you wish – but don't cook them with the meat!

Dish roast vegetables, and cook and dish green vegetables. Make gravy – see page 149, adding any juices from the roasting tin. Serve with mint sauce – see page 152 or bought mint jelly.

5   VEGETARIAN MAIN COURSES

Two 'real' vegetarian meals, so that the fast growing ranks of vegetarians don't feel left out, and to convince meat eaters how delicious vegetarian food can be. There are also recipes in 'Simply Super' and 'Posher Nosh', marked with the carrot symbol, which give easy alternatives or adaptations for a vegetarian meal. The recipes all use 'normal' ingredients, so that non-veges (both cooks and diners!) won't get too great a shock at having a meatless meal – they probably won't notice if you don't tell them!

SAUCY VEGETABLE PANCAKES

An acceptable main course for non vegetarians too, as it's very tasty and quite substantial. Make and fill the pancakes in advance, put into the fridge, or freeze and defrost them overnight ready to cook in the oven, timed to be ready when you want to eat. A potato dish that can be cooked in the oven with the pancakes, such as cheesy scalloped potatoes and a green vegetable cooked at the last minute, complete the main course.

Preparation time: 35 mins., plus 35 mins. for tomato sauce or 5 mins. for avocado sauce.
Cooking time: 15–30 mins. depending on size of dish.

Pancake batter: **6 oz/150g/6 heaped tblsp plain flour**
       Pinch salt
       2 eggs
       ¾ pint/450ml milk
       Oil for frying
Filling: **2 large onions**
       1–2 cloves garlic or ½ tsp garlic powder
       2 carrots
       12 oz/300g mushrooms
       8 oz/250g fresh beansprouts
       2 tblsp oil for frying
       4–6 tblsp cashew nuts
       2 tblsp soy sauce
1 pint/600ml homemade tomato sauce – see page 151 *and*
2 tblsp Parmesan cheese
or **1 quantity avocado sauce – see page 154**

Make 12 pancakes: Put flour and salt into a bowl, beat in eggs and gradually beat in milk to make a smooth batter (use a mixer or wooden spoon). Heat a clean frying pan over a moderate heat, grease with a little oil and pour in just enough batter to cover pan thinly. Fry until just set on top and lightly browned underneath, shaking pan to stop pancakes sticking. Toss or flip pancake over with a knife, and fry for a further minute to brown other side. Turn pancake onto a plate. Wipe pan with kitchen paper, re-grease and make 12 pancakes.

Make filling: Peel and slice onions, peel and finely chop garlic, peel carrots and cut into tiny matchsticks, wash and slice mushrooms, rinse beansprouts in cold water and drain. Heat oil in a large frying pan or wok over a moderate heat, and fry onion, garlic and carrot sticks for 4–5 minutes until just softened but not mushy. Add mushrooms and cook for a further 5–8 minutes until mushrooms are soft. Stir in cashew nuts and beansprouts and season to taste with soy sauce, salt and pepper.

Lay pancakes out on a clean work surface and divide mixture between them. Roll up or fold into quarters, and place in a large ovenproof dish or 2 smaller dishes.

Tomato pancakes: Pour tomato sauce over pancakes, sprinkle with parmesan cheese, cover with foil and put in fridge or freezer.

Avocado pancakes: Pour sauce over, cover with foil and put in fridge until time to cook, or freeze without sauce (it may curdle), defrosting and covering with sauce before cooking.

To cook: Heat oven at 180°C/350°F/gas 4–5. Bake pancakes, covered with foil, on the top oven shelf above the potatoes for

15–20 minutes – smaller dishes

20–30 minutes – large dish

until cooked right through, timed to be ready when you want to eat.

CREAMY MUSHROOM PUFFS

Absolutely delicious, our vegetarian favourite, so it had to be included. The sauce is very rich, making it a more substantial dish than it may appear. Lovely served with tiny new potatoes, or a potato dish cooked in the oven, (Cheesy Scallops go well) and a plain green vegetable.

Preparation and cooking time: 30 mins.
Finishing time: 5 mins.

6 frozen vol-au-vent cases – large size cases
Little milk for brushing

Filling:
1 lb/500g button mushrooms
1 lb/500g champignons (dark coloured mushrooms) or field mushrooms
2–3 cloves garlic or ½ tsp garlic granules
2 oz/50g butter and 1 tblsp olive or cooking oil

1 pint/600ml altogether { **½ pint/300ml plain yoghurt, soured cream or crème fraiche** **½ pint/300ml double cream** }
Salt, pepper

Fresh parsley/and/or watercress to garnish

Heat the oven at 210°C/425°F/gas 7–8. Put 6 frozen vol-au-vent cases onto a baking sheet – no need to grease – brush with milk and bake in the hot oven for 10 minutes or as instructed on the packet, until risen and pale golden. Put on a wire tray to cool, and remove little round tops, using a vegetable knife, and save for decoration. You should now have 6 flaky pastry cases; it doesn't matter if they've fallen over a bit during baking.

Make filling: Wash and slice mushrooms, peel and chop garlic. Heat butter and oil in a large saucepan over a moderate heat and fry mushrooms and garlic gently for 6–8 minutes, stirring frequently, until cooked. Remove mushrooms and put into a basin, leaving the juice in the pan – there will be lots of juice. Return pan to heat and bring the juice to the boil and cook rapidly for a few minutes to reduce the liquid, leaving 3–4 tblsp sauce. Put aside until ready to serve.

To serve: Reheat pastry puffs in the oven for 2–3 minutes and keep warm. Heat mushrooms and reduced sauce in the pan over a gentle heat, stirring carefully until really hot and heated right through, not just warmed.

Stir in chosen cream mixture and continue heating gently until sauce is hot but not boiling (it may curdle if it gets too hot). Season with salt and pepper.

Put a hot pastry case onto each plate and fill to over flowing with mushrooms and sauce. Top with a pastry lid, garnish with rinsed fresh snipped parsley and/or a little bunch washed watercress, and serve at once.

6   VEGETABLES AND VEGETABLE DISHES

POTATOES

People always seem to eat more at dinner parties when they're sitting round talking – it's easy to have a second helping while you're enjoying yourself – so I prefer to err on the generous side with the amounts of vegetables: I'd rather have a few potatoes left over than run out. Remember too, it's the helpings of potatoes which reveal the real difference in appetites, so adjust your amounts accordingly, depending on whether you're catering for the rowing eight, hungry students, the neighbours, sophisticated business colleagues or Granny, Grandpa, and your figure-conscious sister.

Allow approximately 6–8 oz/200–250g/2–4 unpeeled raw potatoes per person, according to size (of potatoes and persons!). If you buy a 3½ lb/1½kg bag of potatoes, just use them all – this will give you six generous helpings. Mashed potatoes never seem to go as far as you expect (maybe the potatoes crumble a little during cooking and you lose some), so allow a little extra at the peeling stage.

Potatoes can be peeled the night before and left in cold water in a cool place overnight. Potatoes can be boiled, mashed or roasted, and dished up and kept warm just before the guests arrive. If you want an easy life, make potato castles or cheesy potatoes the night before or earlier and freeze them, ready to heat just before eating; or prepare a potato dish, Scalloped Potatoes or Ki's Special Potatoes, etc., earlier in the day, which will only require putting into the oven timed to be ready with the main course.

Boiled Potatoes: Can be prepared just before the guests arrive, dished and kept warm in a very low oven (100°C/200°F/gas ½–1). Peel as thinly as possible, dig out eyes and black bits, cut large potatoes in halves or quarters, and simmer in boiling, salted water for 15–20 minutes until just soft when tested with a knife. Drain and serve garnished with washed, snipped parsley.

Mashed Potatoes: Prepare and boil as above. When soft, drain well and mash with a fork or masher until lump-free and fluffy. Heap into a serving dish, garnish and keep warm as above.

Creamed Potatoes: Prepare mashed potatoes, then beat in 2 oz/50g butter and 1–2 tblsp top-of-the-milk. Fork into a heap on a serving dish, garnish and keep warm as above.

Cheesy Potatoes: Prepare creamed potatoes as above. Grate 8 oz/250g mature Cheddar cheese, and beat it into the potato, saving a little for topping. Well grease an ovenproof dish and pile potato mixture into the dish. Fork down evenly and top with the remainder of the grated cheese. Put aside until needed, or freeze and defrost overnight before cooking. To bake: heat the oven at 200°C/400°F/gas 6–7, and bake for 15–20 minutes until crisp and golden.

Potato Castles or Easy Duchesse Potatoes: Prepare creamed potatoes; you can beat in one or two spare egg yolks left over from any pudding you may have made and reduce the amount of milk. Grease a flat baking tray and pile potatoes in even-sized heaps, allowing 2 or 3 castles per person. Fork into castles and top with a dab of butter. Put aside. To serve: heat the oven at 200°C/400°F/gas 6–7, and bake the castles for 10–15 minutes until crisp and golden. You can prepare them in advance, or freeze them uncooked and defrost them for 2 to 3 hours or overnight, ready to cook in the oven while eating the starter.

Parsnip Castles: An unusual mixture with a lovely taste. Prepare as potato castles, but use half potatoes and half parsnips, peeled, boiled and mashed together.

New Potatoes: So easy, no peeling! Choose potatoes of approximately equal size or cut large potatoes in half. Wash potatoes well and scrub with a pan scrubber, removing any eyes or black bits. Boil in lightly salted water with a sprig of mint for 15-20 minutes according to size, until just soft. Drain and keep warm. Serve garnished with a few sprigs of fresh mint and a large dab of butter.

Roast Potatoes: Always popular, served with casseroles as well as the traditional joint, and easy to cook in the oven with the main course. Heat the oven at 200°C/400°F/gas 6–7. Peel potatoes and cut into even-sized pieces. Cook in boiling, salted water for 3-5 minutes. Put enough fat (vegetable oil or dripping) to cover the base of the roasting tin, and heat it in the oven while the potatoes are par boiling. Drain potatoes well, shake them in the pan over the heat for a few moments to dry thoroughly, then put into the hot roasting tin (watch out for fatty splashes), and roast at the top of the oven for 45–60 minutes, until golden brown and crispy.

If roasting a joint, the par boiled potatoes can be put into the hot roasting tin and cooked round the joint for the last ¾–1 hour of cooking time. If cooking a casserole on a lower heat, put this on the lowest shelf and the roasting tin of potatoes at the top, turning up the heat to cook the potatoes.

Jacket Potatoes: Allow 1 or 2 whole potatoes per person, according to appetite. It's easier to cook medium-sized rather than enormous potatoes which take ages to cook. Wash and well scrub 6–12 even-sized medium potatoes and prick several times with a fork. If you like a softer skin, wrap each potato loosely in cooking foil. The cooking time is very flexible, according to what else is cooking in the oven, the size of the potatoes and whether foil-wrapped, so cook approximately for:

1–1½ hours at 200°C/400°F/gas 6–7 unwrapped
1¼–1¾ hours at 200°C/400°F/gas 6–7 wrapped in foil
1½–2 hours at 170°C/325–350°F/gas 3–5 unwrapped or par
    boil in hot water for 10–15 minutes and then bake for
    30–45 minutes at 200°C/400°F/gas 6–7 unwrapped.

Serve plain, piled into a hot serving dish, or make a slit in the top of each potato and pop in a knob of cold butter or a little cream cheese, or serve these separately. The potatoes can be kept hot in a low oven (100°C/200°F/gas ½–1) until ready to serve.

Baked Stuffed Potatoes: Make in advance and heat at the last minute. Wash and bake 6 medium/large jacket potatoes as above. When soft, remove from oven and cut in half lengthwise, scooping all the soft potato out into a bowl. Mash with a fork and mix in 2 oz/50g butter, 6 oz/150g grated mature Cheddar cheese, salt and pepper. Pile filling back into the potato skins and fork down attractively. Place on a baking sheet and put aside until needed.

To serve: heat the oven at 200°C/400°F/gas 6–7, and bake stuffed potatoes for 10–15 minutes until crisp and golden – they can be cooked while you are eating the starter.

POTATO DISHES

A big dish of potatoes prepared in advance and popped into the oven an hour or so before your guests are due is an easy way of serving potatoes and saves a lot of last-minute dashing around draining steaming pans. If you're serving a casserole which is already in the oven on a lower heat than the potatoes will need, put the casserole onto the lowest shelf of the oven, put the potatoes on the top shelf and raise the oven temperature to suit the potatoes; the casserole will continue to cook more slowly lower down. If you haven't got a large enough dish – one that holds about 5 pints/3 litres and is 2"/5cm deep is ideal – use two smaller dishes of a similar depth or buy a large foil dish. Calculate the cooking time so that the potatoes are cooked when you want to dish up the meal.

SCALLOPED POTATOES

An easy way of serving potatoes. Prepare in advance and

cook timed to be ready with the main course.

Preparation time: 10 mins.
Cooking time: 1½–2 hours, large dish. 1–1½ hours, small dishes.

3 lb/1½kg potatoes
2 tblsp flour
Salt, pepper, a little butter
¾ pint/½ litre approx. milk – you can use single cream or
half and half if you feel extravagant, it's very
rich but absolutely delicious

Heat the oven at 200°C/400°F/gas 6–7. Grease a large ovenproof dish very well. Peel potatoes and slice thinly. Put a layer of potato slices into the dish, sprinkle with a tsp flour, salt and pepper, and repeat layers until the dish is full and all the potatoes are used up. Add enough milk and/or cream almost to cover the potatoes, dot with butter. Put aside.

To cook, put into the hot oven for 1–2 hours, until the milk is absorbed and the potatoes are crisp on top and soft underneath – cover lightly with a piece of foil if they seem to be getting too brown.

This dish can be cooked and then kept warm in a low oven (100°C/200°F/gas ½–1) while you are eating the starter.

CHEESY SCALLOPS
Grate 6 oz/150g mature Cheddar Cheese and sprinkle over each layer of potato with the flour, and sprinkle a little on the top (omit butter) to give a nice, crispy topping. Bake and serve as before.

HERB SCALLOPS
Wash and finely scissor-snip a large handful of fresh

parsley and/or chives over the potato layers with the flour. Bake and serve as above.

ONION SCALLOPS
Peel and finely chop 2 large onions, and scatter over each layer of potatoes with the flour. Bake and serve as above.

POMMES BOULANGER

A quickly prepared, substantial but not too rich, savoury potato dish. Prepare in advance and cook in the oven, timed to be ready with the main course.

Preparation time: 15 mins.
Cooking time: 1½–2 hours large dish, 1–1½ hours small dishes.

3 lb/1½kg potatoes
2 medium onions
3–4 tomatoes
3 tblsp flour
Salt, pepper
1 stock cube – beef, chicken or vegetable according
　to the main course
¾ pint/450ml hot water
1 oz/25g butter

Heat the oven at 200°C/400°F/gas 6–7. Peel and thinly slice potatoes. Peel and finely chop onions. Wash and slice tomatoes. Put a layer of potato slices into a well greased ovenproof dish (or dishes), scatter with chopped onion and sliced tomato, flour, salt and pepper. Repeat the layers, finishing with a layer of potato. Dissolve stock cube in the hot water and pour over potato mixture, using enough almost to cover the potatoes. Dot with a little butter and put aside until needed.

To bake, cook in the hot oven for 1–2 hours until brown and crispy and potatoes are soft underneath; cover with a piece of foil if they seem to be getting too brown. Can be kept warm until needed in a very low oven (100°C/200°F/gas ½–1).

KI'S SPECIAL POTATOES

My youngest son's favourite. Easy to make and quite substantial; there are so many vegetables in the recipe that you only need a plain green vegetable to complete the meal with the main course.

Preparation time: 20 mins.
Cooking time: 1½–2 hours large dish, 1–1½ hours small dishes.

3 lb/1½kg potatoes
2 large onions
1 small green pepper
1 small red pepper
6 oz/150g Cheddar or Edam cheese
1 heaped tblsp flour
Handful fresh parsley and/or fresh chives
Salt, pepper
¾ pint/½ litre (approx.) milk
Butter for topping

Heat the oven at 200°C/400°F/gas 6–7. Well grease a large ovenproof dish, or two smaller dishes. Peel potatoes and cut into ½"/1cm dice. Peel and chop onions, wash, de-seed and chop peppers. Mix vegetables together in a large bowl. Grate cheese and stir into the veg with the flour, washed snipped herbs, salt and pepper. Turn the mixture into the greased dish and pour over enough milk so that it almost covers them. Dot with butter and put aside until required.

To cook, put into the hot oven and bake for 1 to 2 hours, depending on size of dish, until the potatoes are golden brown on top and all the vegetables are cooked – cover lightly with foil if it seems to be getting too brown. Time it so that the potatoes are ready with the main course.

PASTA

Allow 3–4 oz/75–100g dry pasta per person, depending on appetite, or more if you're entertaining the rugby team. I would cook 1½ lb/750g dry pasta for six generous servings.

Pasta can be a bit tricky to serve at a formal dinner party, as it is best cooked just before eating; it goes sticky if left waiting too long. So, either cook pasta just before you serve the starter, or cut out the first course and just serve drinks and nibbles in the kitchen. Undercook pasta slightly, drain well and then rinse in boiling water to get rid of the sticky starch. Drain again, and keep warm in a very low oven (100°C/200°F/gas ½–1) until ready to finish and serve.

Alternatively, use fresh pasta, which only takes a few minutes to cook, and actually cook it between courses. Have the kettle boiled, large saucepan ready, and the rest of the main course dished up. Cook fresh pasta in boiling, salted water with a tsp vegetable oil for 2–3 minutes (enquire about exact cooking time when you buy it), drain and serve at once.

Dry pasta will have the cooking instructions on the packet. It is generally cooked in a large saucepan of boiling, salted water with a tsp vegetable oil to stop the pasta sticking to the pan. Put pasta into well boiling water (stand long spaghetti in the pan and push it down as it softens), let the water come back to the boil, then lower heat and leave to simmer without a lid, or it will boil over, for:–

10–12 minutes – dry wholemeal pasta
8–10 minutes – dry white pasta
2–4 minutes – fresh pasta.

Pasta should be al dente, not too soft, when cooked. Drain cooked pasta well in a colander, then return to the dry pan and toss in a little butter, yoghurt, cream or soured cream. Tip into a warm serving dish and top with a handful of washed, snipped parsley or chives, or 1–2 tblsp chopped nuts – walnuts, cashews or pine kernels, or a shake of paprika pepper.

RICE

Can be cooked just before your guests arrive: under cook slightly, drain well and fluff with a fork to separate the grains, and keep warm in a very low oven, (100°C/200°F/gas ½–1) covered lightly with foil, until ready to serve.

Use long grain or patna type rice for savoury dishes; the smaller round grain rice is used for puddings. Brown rice, the equivalent of wholemeal bread, takes longer to cook than white, otherwise they are prepared and served exactly the same.

Easy cook rice is also widely available and is simple to prepare. Cooking instructions are usually given on the packet for all types of rice, and should be followed exactly to get the best results for that particular type of rice.

There are numerous methods of cooking rice, but when cooking a large amount for a dinner party I prefer to use the following method, using a large pan and lots of water –

I find with some methods of cooking rice in a very little water it's too nerve-racking trying to catch the pan before it boils dry.

Preparation and cooking time: 15 mins. for white rice
   35 mins. for brown rice.

Allow 2–4 oz/50–100g dry rice per person, according to appetite, and whether you're catering for slimming girl friends or several hungry men! I would use 1½ lb/750g dry rice for six generous portions.

Put chosen rice in a large saucepan and rinse well in several rinses of cold water to get rid of excess starch. Drain, and put rice into a very large saucepan. Pour on boiling water to come two-thirds up the pan. Add 1 tsp salt, bring back to the boil and simmer with the lid off the pan for:–

10–12 minutes white rice
25–30 minutes brown rice

until rice is just *al dente*, (or slightly undercooked if you are going to keep it hot). Do not overcook or it will go sticky and puddingy. Drain very well, fluff with a fork to separate the grains, and tip gently into a warm serving dish and fluff again. Garnish with a little washed, snipped parsley. Cover lightly with a large piece of foil and keep warm until needed. The rice can be served on a large serving platter, moulded into a deep ring, with the curry or casserole poured inside.

VEGETABLES

Vegetables complete the main course and are a most important part of the meal. For a dinner party, choose vegetables or vegetable dishes that can be prepared in advance or quickly and easily cooked at the last minute; you just haven't time to fuss over vegetables in the middle of a dinner party.

Choose vegetables to accompany a meal like an artist completing a picture. Pick them for their variety, taste, colour and texture, to complement the rest of the main course. If serving several veg., choose different kinds – a leafy veg. such as broccoli, beans, peas or carrots, and perhaps one vegetable dish to provide a sauce, bearing in mind the resulting colour combinations and the type of main course, potatoes, pasta or rice going with them. Forget vegetables in fancy sauces, it takes too much last-minute effort, save that for a quiet dinner *à deux* – a knob of butter or tub of yoghurt or cream is an easy, delicious alternative. If in doubt, play safe and serve a green salad – that goes with everything, hot or cold, meat, fish or vegetarian meal, and can be prepared in advance to save any last-minute panic.

Another easy way of dealing with 'the vegetables', is to serve a vegetable dish which can be prepared in advance and just put into the oven timed to be ready with the main course. A casserole or roast and a vegetable dish can be cooked together in the oven, with whichever dish needs the hottest temperature on the top shelf. There are some tasty vegetable recipes suggested in the menus.

Frozen vegetables are a great help when cooking for larger numbers; they are ready prepared and quickly cooked. But beware of overcooking; manufacturers seem to recommend boiling their products for far too long, and it is better to undercook the vegetables slightly if they are to be kept warm while you are eating the starter. Do be aware of the fresh vegetables available; it seems silly to buy a bag of frozen cauliflower sprigs when (for half the price) you could buy a big, fresh white cauli which will take very little preparation, look marvellous and taste super.

Buy best quality vegetables, find out what is in season, and try to include some fresh vegetables in the menu if possible. Discard or refuse bruised or damaged fresh vegetables or frozen packets covered in frost that look as if they've been at the bottom of the freezer for months. Remember that you need something plain to balance a rich meal, and some of your guests may prefer the more familiar vegetables – carrots, cabbage or sprouts – and there's always someone who only likes frozen peas!! Plain vegetables complement a spicy main course, and you certainly don't need 'fancy' potatoes and vegetables at the same meal. So, mix and match – fresh and frozen, plain, exotic and saucy – and you'll have a lovely meal.

Fresh Vegetables

Choose fresh vegetables according to season – if you're not sure what's 'in' just take a good look round the green-grocery counter and see what looks fresh and good value for money. Lots of vegetables are now available all year round, but 'out of season' they may be imported and very expensive. You can mix and match fresh and frozen veg in the same dish – fresh carrot rings mixed with frozen peas, or a small quantity of expensive mangetout peas mixed with frozen petit pois for example; and remember, if you're serving several vegetables you won't need quite so much of each. You will obviously have your favourites, and may want to try out different vegetables you see in the supermarket, but below is a brief list of some of the easiest fresh vegetables to cook for a dinner party, which don't need too much fuss at the last minute and can be safely left to keep warm while eating the starter.

Prepare fresh vegetables in advance, all ready to cook when needed – I prepare them the night before, put into saucepans or covered bowls (not in water or all the taste will soak out), and leave in a cool place until needed (the garage makes a good larder, it's nice and cold).

Allow extra weight when buying fresh vegetables, according to the amount of wastage in peeling or preparing. Allow approximately 4–8 oz/100–250g unprepared vegetables per serving, according to type, e.g. 1½ lb/¾kg new carrots or new French beans for 6 people, but 2 lb/1kg broccoli or sprouts and 3 lb/1½kg broad beans.

GREEN BEANS: French or runner: allow 1½–2 lb/¾–1kg. Top and tail, string or slice if necessary. Cook in a little boiling salted water for 5–10 minutes, until *al dente*. Drain and serve with a big dab of butter.

BROAD BEANS: Allow 3 lb/1½kg. Pod beans, cook in boiling, salted water for 5–8 minutes, until just soft. Drain and serve, topped with butter and fresh, snipped parsley.

BROCCOLI: Allow 2 lb/1kg, or 2–3 sprigs per person. Cut off tough outer leaves and end of stalks. Boil in a little salted water for 5 minutes until soft. Drain well, and serve with a knob of butter or topped with a little plain yoghurt.

BRUSSELS SPROUTS: Allow 2 lb/1kg. Choose small, fresh-looking even-sized sprouts. Cut off stalks, trim outer leaves, wash well. Cook in boiling salted water for 5–10 minutes, drain well and serve sprinkled with a few split almonds if liked.

CABBAGE: Use 1 medium white or green cabbage, approx. 2 lb/1kg – it goes a long way, but boils down less as it cooks. Trim outer leaves and stalk, shred and wash well. Cook for 3–5 minutes in *very* little boiling, salted water, being careful not to overcook. Drain well.

CARROTS: Allow 1½ lb/¾kg. Scrub small, new carrots and leave whole. Peel old carrots and cut into rings or matchsticks, or leave whole. Cook in a little boiling, salted water, with 1 tsp sugar and a large knob of butter for 5–20 minutes, according to size. Serve with the buttery sauce poured over (there will be just a little left in the pan), and sprinkle with washed snipped parsley.

PEAS AND CARROTS: Prepare carrot rings as above. When carrots are almost cooked, add 1 lb/400g frozen peas and continue cooking for 2–3 minutes – you may need to add a little more boiling water with the peas. Drain and serve together.

CAULIFLOWER: Choose a large, firm, white cauli – it should be heavy and thick. Trim stalk and outer leaves, wash very thoroughly, and cook in boiling, salted water for 15–20 minutes. Drain well. Transfer carefully to a serving dish and top with a little plain yoghurt, soured cream or crème fraiche. You may prefer to cut cauli into florets before cooking as above, but they will only take 5–10 minutes to cook. Serve as above.

COURGETTES: Allow 1½ lb/¾kg or 1–2 courgettes each. Wash, top and tail and cut into 1″/2cm slices. Cook gently in a very little boiling, salted water for 2–5 minutes. Drain very well, and serve topped with butter or yoghurt, and a handful of snipped chives or parsley.

MANGETOUT: Delicious and different, but quite expensive. Mix with frozen petit pois to make them go further. Allow 1½ lb/¾kg if serving on their own, or mix 8 oz/250g mangetout with 1 lb/½kg frozen petit pois to serve 6 people. Top and tail and wash pods, cook whole in a little boiling, salted water with a sprig of mint, for 2–3 minutes – they should still be slightly crunchy when cooked. Drain and serve, topped with a knob of butter and a few sprigs of mint. If mixing mangetout and petit pois, the two can be cooked together.

ROAST ONIONS: Allow 1 large onion per person. Spanish onions are excellent. Choose even-sized onions, and cook them separately or in the roasting tin with roast potatoes. Heat oven at 200°C/400°F/gas 6–7, and heat a little oil in a roasting tin. Top and tail and peel onions, and carefully sit onions in the hot tin – beware of splashes. Roast for ¾–1 hour, timing them to be ready to dish up with the main course.

PARSNIPS: Allow 1½ lb/¾kg or 1–2 parsnips per person. Prepare and roast as potatoes – see page 83. Cut large parsnips in half. They go brown very quickly when peeled, so keep them in a pan of cold water with a little lemon juice until ready to cook. Can be cooked separately or in the tin with roast potatoes and onions.

SWEDES: Allow 2 medium-sized swedes for 6 people. Peel thickly, removing all the hard skin. Cut into ½"/1cm chunks. Cook in boiling, salted water for 15–20 minutes until soft. Drain well, return to pan and mash with a potato masher or mixer, adding 1–2 oz (25–50g) butter and lots of freshly ground black pepper. Heap into a serving dish, garnish with parsley sprigs – can be kept warm until needed.

Frozen Vegetables

Some frozen vegetables are more successful than others! They are best cooked at the last minute or just before you serve the starter, and are nicest cooked in a very little, lightly salted water for a few minutes, just long enough to make them tender and heat them right through. This way of cooking preserves the most flavour and goodness, which is lost if the vegetables are cooked in lots of water. Undercook slightly, as they will carry on cooking in their own heat if kept warm before serving.

Allow approx. 3–4 oz/75–100g frozen vegetables per serving, being a little more generous if you are only serving one vegetable and your guests have big appetites!

I would use an 18 oz/500g packet frozen vegetables for 6 people if serving several different vegetables or a little more if only serving one kind.

My preferred frozen vegetables are:

PEAS: Cook in a little boiling, salted water with a sprig of fresh mint, for 2–3 minutes. Drain, stir in 1 tsp sugar, and serve topped with a knob of butter and a few sprigs of fresh mint.

BROCCOLI: Simmer in boiling, salted water in a large pan, until just *al dente* (2–4 minutes). Drain well, and serve in a large, shallow serving dish, topped with butter or a little crème fraiche or plain yoghurt.

FRENCH BEANS: Cook in a little boiling, salted water, until *al dente* – not long, 2–4 minutes. Drain well, serve topped with a large knob of butter and some fresh, snipped parsley.

BRUSSELS SPROUTS: Buy tiny 'button' sprouts if possible. Cook in boiling, salted water for 3–4 minutes, depending on size, but do not overcook or they go soggy. Serve sprinkled with a handful of split almonds if liked.

BROAD BEANS: Cook in a little boiling, salted water for 3–4 minutes, until just soft. Drain and serve with a large pat of butter and fresh snipped parsley, or a dollop of plain or chive yoghurt or crème fraiche, and parsley.

VEGETABLE DISHES

COURGETTE AND TOMATO BAKE 🔥 S 🍽

Make this in the summer when courgettes and tomatoes are cheap and plentiful. Can be prepared in advance and baked just before serving.

Preparation time: 15 mins. Cooking time: 25–30 mins.

1½ lb/680g courgettes
Juice of ½ lemon or 1 tblsp lemon juice
1 lb/500g ripe tomatoes or 14 oz/397g can tomatoes
1–2 cloves garlic or ½ tsp garlic granules

(continued overleaf)

(Courgette and Tomato Bake continued)

Salt, pepper, ½ tsp sugar
2 slices/2 oz/50g fresh bread – white or brown
2 oz/50g butter with 1 tsp vegetable oil
3–4 tblsp grated Parmesan cheese
To garnish – 2–3 lemon slices, sprigs fresh parsley

Heat the oven at 190°C/375°F/gas 5–6. Wash, top and tail and slice courgettes into ½"/1cm slices. Put into a large, deep ovenproof dish or large pie dish. Sprinkle with lemon juice. Wash and chop fresh tomatoes, peel and finely chop or crush fresh garlic, mix together and spoon over courgettes (or add tinned tomatoes and garlic granules). Season with salt, pepper and sugar.

Make breadcrumbs – use a blender or grater. Heat butter and oil in a frying pan over a moderate heat and fry gently for 1–2 minutes until soft and golden. Sprinkle Parmesan cheese on top of tomatoes and top with the breadcrumbs.

Put aside until needed, then bake in the hot oven for 25–30 minutes until the vegetables are cooked (the tomato juices make a nice sauce), and the top is golden and crispy. Decorate with lemon slices and fresh parsley.

MUSHROOMS À LA GRECQUE

Prepare in advance and cook in the oven so that it's timed to be ready with the main meal. Try and use the lovely aromatic Greek olive oil for this dish.

Preparation time: 20 mins. Cooking time: 40–45 mins.

1 lb/½kg mushrooms

2 large onions
2 cloves garlic or ½ tsp garlic granules
2 tblsp olive oil
1 vegetable stock cube
¼ pint/150ml hot water
1 sherry-glass dry white wine or cider
2 tblsp tomato purée or ketchup
1 tsp mixed dried herbs
Salt, pepper
Handful fresh parsley and/or chives
Paprika or cayenne pepper for garnish

Heat the oven at 170°C/325°F/gas 3–4. Wash and slice large mushrooms, (leave button ones whole), and put into a large, deep ovenproof dish. Peel and thinly slice onions, finely chop or crush garlic. Heat oil in a pan over a gentle heat, and fry onion and garlic for 4–5 minutes until soft. Pour over the mushrooms. Dissolve stock cube in hot water, add wine or cider, tomato purée or ketchup and mixed herbs and pour over vegetables. Season with salt and pepper and sprinkle with washed snipped parsley and/or chives. Cover and put aside until the calculated time to cook.

To cook: Put dish, uncovered, into the moderate oven, and bake for 40–45 minutes until the vegetables are soft. Sprinkle with a little paprika or cayenne pepper (according to taste), and serve hot.

SAVOURY RED CABBAGE

A substantial vegetable dish with an intriguing sweet and sour flavour. Best served with plain potatoes – jacket, boiled or roast – or plain noodles, as an accompaniment to the main course. Can be prepared in advance and left ready to cook in time for dinner.

Preparation time: 15 mins. Cooking time: 1½ hours.

2 large onions
1 red cabbage – 2¼ lb/1kg approx.
2–3 eating apples
1 tblsp vegetable oil
Salt, pepper
3 tblsp sugar – brown if possible
3 tblsp vinegar
¼ pint/150ml/1 cup boiling water

Heat oven at 180°C/350°F/gas 4–5. Peel and chop onions. Cut stalk from cabbage, removing any battered outside leaves, then wash and shred cabbage. Peel, core and slice apples. Heat oil in a pan over a moderate heat, and fry onion gently for 3–4 minutes until softened. Using a large casserole or deep ovenproof dish (4–5 pints/ 2–3 litres), put layers of cabbage, apple and onion into the dish, seasoning each layer with salt, pepper, sugar and vinegar. (The dish can now be put aside until it's time to put it in the oven.)

To cook: Pour ¼ pint/150ml/1 cup boiling water over the vegetables, cover with a lid or piece of foil and cook in the hot oven for about 1½ hours, stirring occasionally. Serve hot.

7 SALADS

GREEN OR MIXED GREEN SALAD 🔲 Ⓢ 🔲

The basic standby vegetable accompaniment, can be served with hot or cold main courses. Prepare earlier in the day, saving last-minute hassle – in fact, the lettuce and other veg can be washed and put ready in the fridge the night before.

Preparation time: 10–15 mins.

Use one kind of lettuce or a mixture of 'designer' lettuces, alone or with other green or salad veg. The pre-packs of mixed lettuces are very useful, as it's more economical than buying several different lettuces (unless you're catering for huge numbers) and they look so pretty in the salad bowl.

1 large lettuce – Cos, Chinese leaf, Webbs or
   'ordinary English' type
or 1–2 large pre-packs of 'designer' lettuce, depending on
   whether you are mixing the lettuce with other veg
1 large onion
3–4 tblsp vinaigrette dressing – see page 154

Wash lettuce, tear or shred leaves and place in salad bowl. Peel and finely slice onion and mix with lettuce. Cover with plastic film and keep cool until ready to serve – do not add dressing until the last minute, or lettuce will go limp.

Other salad vegetables can be added to the lettuce, using just green vegetables for a Green Salad, or a mixture, as you prefer.

Celery – washed, scraped, cut into 1″/2cm lengths
Cucumber – washed, cut into rings or chunks
Mustard and cress ⎱
Watercress   ⎰ washed and drained
Spring onions – wash, cut off roots and yellow leaves,
   leave whole or cut into rings
Peppers – washed, de-seeded, cut into thin rings
Tomatoes – washed, cut into slices or quartered
Radishes – top and tail, wash, cut into rings or
   leave whole
Fresh green herbs – parsley, chives, mint (very strong
   flavour), tarragon, thyme, Rosemary – wash and
   scissor-snip finely over salad
To serve: Toss salad well in vinaigrette dressing, or serve the dressing separately.

TOMATO SALAD

Very quick and simple, but brightens up a buffet table and is cheap to make when tomatoes are plentiful – especially if you grow your own or have neighbours who do! Good with a hot or cold main course, or served as a starter with bread rolls and butter.

Preparation time: 10 mins. Standing time: at least 1 hour.

1 lb/500g tomatoes
2 or 3 spring onions or 1 small onion
6 tblsp vinaigrette dressing – see page 154
1 tsp sugar
Pinch garlic powder (optional)
Handful fresh green herbs – parsley, chives, tarragon,
    or Rosemary, any mixture

Wash and thinly slice tomatoes, and arrange slices in a wide, shallow serving dish. Wash, top and tail and finely chop spring onions, or peel and very finely chop small onion, and sprinkle over tomatoes. Mix vinaigrette with the extra sugar and garlic powder if used, and spoon dressing over the tomatoes. Wash and finely scissor-snip chosen herbs over the top. Cover with plastic film and leave in a cool place for at least an hour to absorb the flavours. We prefer tomatoes at room temperature, but you may prefer the salad chilled in the fridge.

POTATO SALAD

Always popular on the buffet table. Can be prepared early and put aside until needed. Delicious made with new potatoes, or use the waxy type of old potatoes that don't break up when cooking.

Preparation and cooking time: 30 mins.

2–2¼ lb/1kg potatoes – new or old
Salt, sprig of mint
3 eggs
¼ pint/150ml mayonnaise
Few sprigs fresh parsley or chives or shake of paprika

Scrub new potatoes or peel old potatoes, and cut into large bite-sized chunks. Cook in gently boiling, salted water with a sprig of mint, for 10–12 minutes, being careful not to let the potato pieces overcook and crumble. Hard boil eggs (simmer in salted water for 10 minutes), plunge eggs into cold water and peel off shells when cool. Cut or slice into 8–10 pieces.

When cooked, drain potatoes, remove mint and rinse in cold water to stop them cooking, then drain really thoroughly. Mix dry potatoes with the mayonnaise and coat well. Carefully mix in the sliced egg, trying not to break them up, and save a few pieces for decoration. Pile mixture into a serving dish, decorate with egg, sprinkle with washed, snipped parsley or chives or a little paprika pepper. Cover with plastic film and put in a cool place until needed.

8 COLD BEGINNINGS

For peace of mind serve a cold starter, then you know you've got no problems with the first course, leaving you free to gulp your sherry while you finish the main course and sort out the vegetables. I once had the unhappy experience of everyone sitting down to the meal when one guest apologised that she couldn't eat melon of all things, so now I keep a fresh grapefruit in the fridge, so that there is a quite acceptable alternative if anyone doesn't like the starter on offer. Canned, drained grapefruit and/or mandarin orange segments, served in a wine glass and decorated with a sprig of fresh mint will make an instant starter too. Make use of bought pâtés – meat, fish and vegetable – now very widely available at delicatessens and supermarkets, and of excellent quality, served on their own or with salad, and lots of hot toast or fresh bread and butter for another quick and easy starter.

CITRUS COCKTAIL   🎃 S 🥕

Prepare in advance and serve well chilled.

Preparation time: 15 mins. Chilling time: 1 hour.

**3 large grapefruit – pink grapefruit look rather special
3 sweet oranges or 1 can mandarine orange segments
1–2 kiwi fruits
2–3 tblsp sugar to taste
6 tblsp sherry (optional)
Few sprigs mint or lemon balm**

Serve in the grapefruit shells or sundae glasses. Cut grapefruit in halves, remove segments, scrape off any white pith and put segments into a bowl. Peel oranges, divide into segments, or drain canned oranges, and mix with grapefruit. Peel and slice or chunk kiwi fruit, add to fruit and mix with sugar to taste. Spoon fruit mixture into grapefruit shells (these look pretty if serrated) or sundae glasses. Pour a spoonful of sherry (if used) over each cocktail and chill until needed. Serve decorated with rinsed sprigs of mint or lemon balm.

MELON – HONEYDEW, CANTALOUP OR OGEN   🎃 S 🥕

The easiest of starters, and always popular, especially when served really chilled on a warm evening. Keep melons in the fridge so that they are well chilled before you cut them. The slices can be prepared in advance and left in the fridge until needed.

Cut Honeydew melons into 4 or 6 canoe-shaped slices,

according to size, and remove seeds with a spoon. Serve melon slices quite plain or place a little sugar and ground ginger on your table for your guests to sprinkle on the melon.

Cantaloup or Ogen melons are smaller and are usually served cut in half to form cups. Scoop out the seeds and give each person half a melon. If you are feeling extravagant you can pour a little port into each melon as you serve them.

Honeymoon Melon Boats with Orange Sails ⓖ Ⓢ 🖾

Preparation time: 15 mins.

1–2 Honeydew melons (according to size)
1–2 large oranges
6 plastic cocktail sticks

Cut 6 equal-sized slices of melon and scoop out seeds with a spoon. Using a vegetable knife cut under the fruit on each slice, separating the flesh from the skin. Then slice fruit (still on the skin) into ½"/1cm strips and push each strip alternately to right and left to make a "long-boat". Cut 6 large round slices from the middle of the oranges and attach them through the cocktail sticks to the boats, to make a "sail" (see fig. 2 overleaf).

Chill in fridge until ready to eat.

Cantaloup or Ogen Melon with Fruit Sorbet ⓖ Ⓢ 🖾

Serve this when these delicious small melons are in season and cheap. They are very sweet and have a different

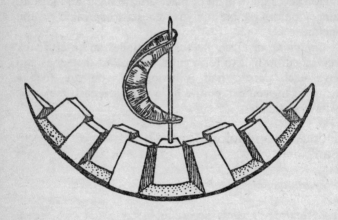

Fig. 2. Melon Boat

flavour and texture from Honeydews. Cheat, and buy a
good fruit sorbet from the supermarket.

Preparation time: 10 mins.

3 Cantaloup or Ogen melons
1 small carton (½ litre size) fruit sorbet – any flavour
    according to taste, but raspberry or lemon is nice.
Few sprigs mint or lemon balm to decorate

Cut the melons in half to make 6 cups – cut with a fancy
V-shaped cut if you feel artistic. Place in sundae glasses
and chill in fridge until needed.
Remove sorbet from freezer and leave to soften in

fridge for 15–30 minutes – according to instructions on pack. When ready to eat, put two or three small scoops of sorbet in each melon half, and decorate with a tiny well-washed sprig of mint or lemon balm.

PARMA HAM   ⬚ ⬚

Buy this Italian cured ham from a good delicatessen where it will be sliced into transparent slices ready to serve. If you prefer, you can serve individual platefuls of Parma ham, garnished with thin rings of red, green or yellow peppers, and black or green olives, or mix Parma ham with other spicy cooked meats, such as Italian or Danish salamis or Garlic sausage. Allow approx. 2 oz/50g sliced cooked meat per serving.

Parma Ham with Melon or Avocado Slices

Preparation time: 10 mins.

12 oz/350g thinly sliced Parma ham
1 large Honeydew melon or 3 ripe avocado pears
4 oz/100g black or green olives
1–2 lemons for garnish and juice

Divide ham into 6 portions. Cut melon in half length-ways and scoop out seeds. Peel carefully, and cut into thin (½"/1cm) slices. Arrange alternate slices of ham and melon on each plate, and garnish with a few olives and a chunk of lemon.
OR
Peel the avocado pears, cut in half and remove stones. Slice each half through from the narrow end nearly to the top, leaving them just joined at the top. Place carefully on

individual plates and open out slices to form a little fan of avocado. Sprinkle with juice of half a lemon to stop them discolouring. Arrange slices of Parma ham on each plate and garnish with olives and a generous slice or chunk of lemon. Chill in the fridge until ready to serve.

AVOCADO PEARS   🍷   S   🏃

The ubiquitous avocado pear – once only served in the best restaurants but now widely available – does add a bit of relatively inexpensive luxury to the menu. The most difficult part of the preparation is in selecting avocados that are just right for eating – not too hard and not too ripe. Forget all those tricks about 'ripening pears in a paper bag in the airing cupboard', they're never ready at the right moment. Buy avocados the day before, just about ready to eat but not too squashy, store them at room temperature and they'll be perfect next day.

Allow half an avocado per person.

Cut avocados in half and remove stone. Brush or sprinkle with lemon juice over all the inside surfaces to prevent browning. Place prepared halves in avocado dishes or on a plate, garnished with a little washed lettuce, cucumber and tomato slices.

Avocado Vinaigrette: Just before serving, spoon a tblsp of vinaigrette dressing (see page 154) into each pear (if you put it in earlier it will run away).

Avocado Mayonnaise: Fill each avocado with a large spoonful of mayonnaise, plain or flavoured with tomato or garlic – see page 112 – as for egg or crab mayonnaise. Cover with plastic film until ready to serve.

Avocado with Cottage Cheese: Use ½ lb/250g tub of cottage cheese – plain, chive, pineapple, etc. to taste – and mix with 3 tblsp mayonnaise. Fill prepared avocado halves with the mixture, heaping it up above the hollow. Garnish with a sprinkle of snipped parsley or a shake of paprika.

Avocado with Tuna: Drain a 7 oz/198g can of tuna fish, and break into pieces, *but do not mash.* Mix ½ lb/250g plain cottage cheese with 3 tblsp mayonnaise, then carefully fold in the tuna pieces. Fill prepared avocado halves with the mixture. Garnish with fresh, snipped chives or parsley.

OEUFS AVOCADO 🖓 S 🇫

An interesting variation on Egg Mayonnaise, without involving raw eggs.

Preparation and cooking time: 20 mins.

6 eggs
½ pint/1 quantity Avocado Sauce (see page 154)
1 small lettuce
½ cucumber
3 large or 6 small tomatoes
1 green or red pepper
Paprika pepper

Hardboil the eggs – simmer for 10 minutes in salted water. Cool in cold water, peel and rinse eggs to get rid of all the shell.

Make avocado sauce (see page 154) and keep in fridge. Wash and dry lettuce, shred finely. Wash and slice cucumber, tomatoes and pepper. Arrange a bed of lettuce on a large serving platter or six individual plates. Slice eggs in rings, or cut in half lengthways and arrange on the lettuce (with cut side down if halved) and arrange cucumber, tomatoes and pepper at side of eggs. Keep in fridge until needed.

To serve, coat the eggs with the avocado sauce, and garnish with a dash of paprika pepper. Serve with thin brown or granary bread and butter.

CRAB AVOCADO 🌱 Ⓢ

Proceed as for Oeufs Avocado, but use 1¼ lb/500g cooked crabmeat instead of the eggs. Cooked crabmeat can be bought fresh or frozen from many supermarkets. If buying frozen crab, allow time for it to defrost thoroughly, preferably in the fridge, before use, and if using fresh crab, buy it the same day and keep it in the fridge until time to serve. You may have a mixture of white and brown crabmeat, which can be mixed together or served separately – try and remove any tiny pieces of shell or cartilage still in the meat.

EGG OR CRAB MAYONNAISE 🌱 Ⓢ

Prepare and serve as for Oeufs or Crab Avocado, using ½ pint/300ml good quality mayonnaise instead of the avocado sauce. If you prefer, stir 1–2 tsp tomato purée or ketchup into the mayonnaise for Oeufs Marie Rose, or mix ½ tsp garlic granules or garlic paste and 1 tblsp thick double cream with the mayonnaise to give a delicious garlic flavour.

FRUIT SALAD SAVOURY 🌱 Ⓢ 🌶

A pleasantly different taste to give a tangy start to a meal. Prepare earlier in the day, and keep in the fridge, spooning into glass goblets or small sundae glasses when ready to serve.

Preparation time: 15 mins.

1 large or 2 small onions, or 6 spring onions
3 sticks celery
Small bunch seedless grapes
2 green eating apples
2 red eating apples
2 large eating pears
1–2 tblsp lemon juice
2 large sweet oranges
4 oz/100g/4 tblsp rough chopped walnut halves
4–6 tblsp vinaigrette dressing (see page 154)
Few sprigs fresh lemon balm, parsley or mint to garnish

Peel onions and cut into thin rings, or wash, trim and slice spring onions. Wash and trim celery, cut into ½"/1cm lengths. Wash seedless grapes. Wash apples (do not peel) cut into quarters, slice into chunks and place in a bowl. Peel, core and slice pears, mix with the apple. Stir in lemon juice and thoroughly coat fruit to stop it browning. Peel oranges, cut into bite-sized pieces, add to fruit in bowl. Add onion, celery, grapes and walnuts to other fruit. Pour over vinaigrette and toss lightly. Cover with plastic film and chill in fridge until needed.

When ready to eat, ladle into individual glasses and garnish with tiny sprigs of washed fresh herbs.

STUFFED TOMATO CUPS   🟥 🆂 🟥

These are good for a summer dinner party when large tomatoes are cheaper and readily available. Prepare the same day and keep in the fridge.

Preparation time: 20 mins.

6 large even-sized tomatoes
1 large/9 oz/250g carton cottage cheese, plain or chive
3 tblsp mayonnaise
Paprika pepper
Salad to garnish – washed, shredded lettuce, cucumber,
   cress, red or green pepper, thinly sliced onion, etc.

Wash and dry tomatoes. Cut a "lid" off the tops (keep for garnish) and scoop out the centre, leaving a thick shell of tomato. Put tomato pulp into a bowl and mix gently with the cottage cheese and mayonnaise, just mixing ingredients, not mashing together. Divide the mixture between the tomato shells (it should be heaped up over the tops). Sprinkle with paprika and cap with the tomato lids at a jaunty angle.

Serve on individual plates, garnished with a little of the chosen salad ingredients, and bread rolls with butter.

BLUE CHEESE PÂTÉ   🔽   S   🎉   ❄

Use any of the many blue cheeses now widely available, Stilton or Danish Blue are probably the cheapest and give a very good flavour. Curd cheese contains less fat (and calories) than full fat cheese, but either is quite suitable. The pâté can be made well in advance and frozen (just remember to allow time for it to defrost on the day!), or made up to 24 hours before and kept in the fridge until needed.

Preparation time: 5 mins. plus at least ½ hour chilling time.

10 oz/250g blue cheese
12 oz/300g curd cheese or full fat cream cheese
3 tblsp milk

3 tblsp dry white wine or cider
Salt, pepper

Garnish:
Fresh fruit – apples, pears, peaches, nectarines, grapes
  Walnut halves, watercress, lemon wedges

Grate or crumble the blue cheese. Put soft cheese into a bowl and beat to a soft cream with the milk and wine. Beat in the blue cheese and season to taste with salt and pepper. Divide mixture in half, and shape each portion into a thick sausage-shape (it's rather sticky but roll lightly with your fingertips, like Plasticine). Wrap each "sausage" in plastic film, and leave in fridge for at least half an hour.

To serve: Cut the pâté into slices and arrange several slices on individual small plates, garnished with fresh fruit slices or little bunches of grapes, or walnut halves and a small bunch of washed, trimmed watercress. Alternatively, serve as a wedge of pâté, with thin, hot toast (which has to be made at the last minute and is nice served in a basket or bowl wrapped loosely in a napkin), or French bread and butter, and garnish with lemon wedges.

The pâté can be frozen after wrapping in plastic film. Allow about an hour for it to defrost before serving, then store in fridge until needed.

POTTED SHRIMPS 🖝

Traditionally made with tiny *fresh* Morecambe Bay shrimps, which taste marvellous but take hours to pick (shell). So, cheat, and use fresh or frozen ready picked shrimps, not prawns. Prepare the same day, allowing time for the butter to cool.

Preparation time: 15 mins.   Cooling time: approx 1 hour.

½ lb/250g butter
1¼ lb/500g fresh or defrosted picked shrimps (weight
   after shelling, allow double weight for unpicked)
Juice of 1 lemon or 2 tblsp fresh lemon juice
Black pepper

Garnish:—
   A little washed shredded lettuce or watercress
   1–2 lemons cut into large wedges
Brown or granary bread or rolls and butter

Clarify the butter – cut butter into pieces, place in a
wide saucepan and melt slowly, do not allow it to boil or
brown. When the butter is a hot liquid, just below boiling
point, carefully pour off the clear golden liquid into a
pyrex or heat-proof jug, leaving the white scum behind in
the saucepan.

Rinse shrimps in cold water in a sieve or colander, drain
well and tip into a basin. Pour in half the clarified butter
and mix well with the lemon juice and a good shake of
freshly ground black pepper – be careful not to break the
shrimps. Divide mixture between 6 ramekins and top each
pot with a layer of the clarified butter, to make a butter
"lid". Put in fridge to cool until ready to serve.

Place ramekins on small plates, garnished with shredded lettuce or watercress, and lemon wedges. I prefer to
serve potted shrimps really cold, but some people prefer
them at room temperature or even warmed very slightly in
the oven for a few moments before serving.

9   HOT STARTERS

Either prepare the dish completely, ready for popping into the oven or heating on top of the stove, or assemble everything for a hot starter before guests arrive (weigh ingredients, put out cooking equipment, grease dishes, prepare garnish etc.) to minimise last-minute preparation time. Until you're sure of yourself, aim for reheating rather than cooking, you'll probably have guests in the kitchen with you, and it's difficult to concentrate on a new recipe while chatting.

And why not cheat a bit – what's wrong with well chosen canned soup when you're in a hurry, titivated with wine or sherry, cream or yoghurt, croûtons if you've time to make them, and sprinkled with fresh snipped herbs? Absolutely nothing at all!

GRILLED GRAPEFRUIT

Much more interesting than plain grapefruit halves. Prepare in advance, place in the grill pan and leave in a cool place until ready to heat and serve.

Preparation and cooking time: 15 mins.

3 large grapefruit
6 tsp demerara sugar (granulated will do if necessary)
6 tsp sherry – dry or sweet (optional)

Cut each grapefruit in half, separate the fruit segments to make eating easy. Place halves in the clean grill pan. Sprinkle each half with 1 tsp sugar and pour 1 tsp chosen sherry, if used, into the centre of each half. Leave until needed.

Heat the grill, then 'toast' the grapefruits for 3–4 minutes, until just warmed through, with a nice brown juicy top. Serve in 'sundae' glasses (be careful not to crack them with the hot fruit), and spoon any extra juice over the top.

CHICKEN BOUCHÉES

An easy cheat, but it looks and tastes good. Cook the pastry in advance, heating through in the oven as your guests arrive.

Preparation and cooking time: 30 mins.
Reheating time: 5 mins.

6 frozen vol-au-vent cases – the large ones
2 large (15 oz/420g) cans chicken in white sauce
Handful of fresh parsley or chives

2–3 tblsp yoghurt or double cream
Salt, black pepper

Heat the oven at 425°F/210°C/gas 7–8, and cook 6 pastry cases as instructed on the packet. When they are cooked, using a pointed vegetable knife, carefully remove the little round tops of the bouchée cases and reserve. Empty chicken sauce into a saucepan, put in fridge. Save 6 sprigs parsley for garnish, wash and scissor-snip rest of parsley or chives.

Reheat oven when your guests arrive. When ready to eat, pop pastry cases into the oven for 3–5 minutes to reheat. Put the pan of chicken over a low heat, and warm through very thoroughly, stirring carefully to stop it catching on the base; do not let it boil. Stir in enough yoghurt or cream to make a thick pouring sauce, and add the snipped herbs. Season to taste with salt and pepper.

Put the hot pastry cases on warm serving plates and fill to overflowing with chicken sauce. Top with pastry lids and garnish with pastry sprigs. Serve at once.

LETTUCE SOUP or

Can be served hot or cold (I prefer it hot so the recipe is in this section!), garnished with cream or yoghurt, fresh parsley and a handful of croûtons if serving hot. You'll need a processor or liquidizer.

Preparation and cooking time: 45 mins.
Reheating time: 5 mins.

1 large onion
3 medium potatoes
1 large lettuce

(continued over)

(Lettuce Soup continued)

1 oz/25g butter and 1 tblsp oil for frying
2 stock cubes – chicken or vegetable
3 pints/1½ litres hot water
Salt, pepper
Croûtons – see page 148
To garnish:–
      5 fl oz/142g carton double cream,
       sour cream or plain yoghurt
      Handful of fresh parsley

Peel and chop onion. Peel and thinly slice potatoes. Wash and shred lettuce. Heat butter and oil in a large saucepan and gently fry onion for 4–5 minutes, stirring frequently until softened. Stir in sliced potatoes and shredded lettuce and mix all together. Dissolve chosen stock cubes in hot water, add to the vegetables in pan, bring to the boil, then reduce heat, cover pan and simmer for 20 minutes, until soft. Cool slightly, then blend in a liquidizer or processor to produce a fairly thick velvety smooth soup. Season to taste with salt and pepper. Cool, then store in fridge.

Make croûtons – see page 148. Wash parsley sprigs.

If serving hot: Heat soup thoroughly, making sure it heats right through. Pour into bowls, stir in a tblsp of cream or yoghurt into each helping, leaving a squirly pattern. Sprinkle with a small handful of croûtons and scissor-snip a little parsley on top. If serving at table from a tureen, heat tureen before pouring in the soup, garnish with cream or yoghurt, but serve the croûtons separately on the table.

If serving cold: Chill soup thoroughly in the fridge for at least 2 hours. Garnish with cream or yoghurt and parsley as above, but omit the croûtons – they can make the soup greasy when cold.

GARLIC MUSHROOMS ON TOAST 🍷 ▨ LM 🐔

A slight hint of garlic wafting from the kitchen gives a good French flavour to your dinner party. Prepare and cook the mushrooms in advance, ready to reheat when making the toast just before serving.

Preparation and cooking time: 10 mins.
Reheating time: 10 mins.

1¼ lb/½kg mushrooms
3–4 cloves fresh garlic or 1 tsp garlic powder or paste
6 oz/150g butter with 6 tsp olive oil or cooking oil
6 thick slices bread (granary is nice). Cut off the
    crusts if you prefer
Handful fresh parsley

Wash mushrooms, slice if very large, otherwise leave whole. Peel, chop and crush fresh garlic if used. Melt butter and oil in a large pan over a moderate heat, add garlic (fresh, powder or paste) and mushrooms. Stir well and fry very gently for 4–5 minutes, spooning the garlic butter over the mushrooms. Remove from heat, cover and keep until needed.

When ready to eat, toast the bread lightly and reheat mushroom mixture gently but thoroughly, stir well and make sure it is really hot not just warmed. Wash and snip parsley into mushrooms.

Put a slice of toast on each plate, spoon the mushrooms onto the toast and pour any remaining garlic butter on top. Serve at once.

BAKED EGGS

Quite an impressive starter, prepared completely in advance and only requiring popping into the pre-heated oven 15 minutes before you want to eat.

Preparation time: 15 mins.   Cooking time: 10–15 mins.

8 oz/250g Cheddar cheese
8 oz/250g mushrooms
6 large fresh eggs – size 1 or 2
6 tblsp plain yoghurt or double cream
Salt, black pepper
2 oz/50g approx. butter
Small granary loaf or 6 granary rolls and butter

Grease 6 ramekin dishes. Grate cheese, divide in half and put one half evenly into the ramekins. Wash and slice mushrooms thinly, and divide between the dishes with the cheese. Break eggs one at a time into a cup, then carefully slide them on top of the cheese and mushrooms. Spoon a little yoghurt or cream over each egg, season well with salt and pepper, sprinkle with rest of cheese and dot with a knob of butter. Put in fridge until ready to cook.

Heat the oven at 180°C/350°F/gas 4–5. Place ramekin dishes on a baking tray, and bake in the moderate oven for 10–15 minutes, until the eggs are set and the cheese is bubbling. Heat bread or rolls in the oven with the ramekins for approximately 5 minutes. Serve baked eggs at once, with hot bread and butter.

HAM AND ASPARAGUS MORNAY
(or)

A more expensive starter, but it can be teamed with a

cheaper main course or pud to even things up. Prepare the same morning, or freeze in advance but defrost overnight before cooking. For vegetarians, omit the ham and serve Asparagus Mornay.

Preparation time: 20 mins.   Cooking time 25–30 mins.

1 pint/600ml cheese sauce
2 cans (10 oz/280g size) asparagus spears (use 3 cans
  if omitting the ham)
6 thin slices of ham (or 3 large thin slices halved)
4 oz/100g grated Cheddar cheese
1–2 heaped tblsp grated Parmesan cheese

Prepare the cheese sauce – see page 150. Grease a deep ovenproof dish (big enough to hold 6 bundles of asparagus). Trim any fat from the ham and divide the asparagus into six equal bundles. Wrap a ham slice around each bundle. Place bundles in the greased dish (use a fish slice to scoop them up), and pour the cheese sauce over the top.

For vegetarians: Put a layer of asparagus in the dish and pour the sauce over the top.

Sprinkle the Parmesan cheese over the cheese sauce, and store in the fridge until 35 minutes before serving or freeze uncooked.

Heat the oven at 200°C/400°F/gas 6–7. Cook in the hot oven for 25–30 minutes until the top is crispy and golden. Serve with bread rolls and butter if you wish, but it's quite a filling starter!

10   PROPER PUDS

Back to the nursery, and school meals with a difference!
You'll be surprised how popular these types of puddings
have become, and how many people will confess to a
secret passion for bread and butter pud or treacle tart.
Many hot puds can be pre-cooked earlier in the day and
warmed through in the oven while you're eating the main
course. Whatever the pud, it is even better if served with a
tempting jug of cream or a bowl of Greek yoghurt, or
crème fraiche.

PEARS IN RED WINE   [🔥] or [V] [S]

A delightfully different dessert; pretty deep pink pears
poached in a boozy syrup. Serve hot or cold.

Preparation time: 10 mins.
Cooking time: 1–1½ hours plus 1–2 hours cooling time.

6 large equal-sized pears
6 tblsp sugar
¼ pint/150ml red wine
¼ pint/150ml water
1 sherry-glass port – or use a miniature bottle
To serve: ½ pint/300ml thick cream or Greek yoghurt

Heat the oven at 170°C/325°F/gas 3–4. Wash, core and peel pears – use a vegetable knife or apple corer to remove core from base of pears, but leave stalk for decoration. Stand peeled pears in a deep ovenproof dish. Put sugar, wine and water into a small saucepan and heat gently, stirring to dissolve sugar, then allow to boil gently for 4–5 minutes to thicken syrup slightly. Stir in port, and pour hot syrup over pears in the dish – it should nearly cover them.

Cook in the low oven, spooning the syrup over pears quite frequently, until pears are soft and a deep pink. Serve in the wine syrup.

If serving cold, chill until needed, or reheat in the low oven while eating the main course if serving hot. Serve cream or Greek yoghurt on the table separately.

HOT PEACH CRUNCH 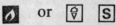 or

A lovely crunchy pud, a mixture between a charlotte and a crumble. When I first made this I was abroad and thought I'd bought a tin of apricots. However, they turned out to be peaches and made a delicious pud; either fruit would be suitable so choose whichever you prefer.

Preparation and cooking time: 50–60 mins.

2 cans (15 oz/420g size) peaches
6 oz/150g/6 slices bread – white or brown
3 oz/75g butter
4 oz/100g sugar
4 oz/100g mixed chopped nuts
To serve: ½ pt/300ml thick cream, crème fraiche or Greek
yoghurt

Heat the oven at 180°C/350°F/gas 4–5. Drain fruit (use
the juice in fruit drinks) and put into a 2½ pint/1½ litre
pie dish or ovenproof dish. Make breadcrumbs (use a
processor or grater). Melt butter in a clean frying pan, stir
in breadcrumbs, sugar and nuts. Mix well, remove from
heat and spoon mixture over fruit. Bake in the moderate
oven for 25–30 minutes, until the nutty topping is golden
and crispy.

To reheat, put into a low oven (150°C/300°F/gas 2–3)
while eating the main course. Serve the chosen cream on
the table separately.

BREAD AND BUTTER PUDDING

Yet another 'school-days' pud enjoying a popular revival –
especially if you can forget the bread and custard horrors
dished out at some school dinners. The proper version is
light, crispy and delicious.

Preparation and soaking time: 45 mins.
Cooking time: 40–45 mins.

6–8 slices white bread
3–4 oz/75–100g butter (it gives a better flavour than
marg.)
4 oz/100g currants or sultanas

4 oz/100g sugar
3 eggs
1 pint/600ml milk

Well grease a 2½ pint/1½litre deep pie or ovenproof
dish. Remove crusts from bread and butter bread thickly.
Cut each slice into 4 triangles and arrange an overlapping
layer of buttered bread on the base of the dish, butter side
down. Wash and drain dried fruit and sprinkle about half
over the bread with 1 tblsp of sugar. Cover with another
layer of bread triangles and repeat with rest of fruit and
another tblsp sugar. Cover with rest of bread, butter side
up, sprinkle with remaining sugar. Beat eggs well, mix in
milk and pour over the pud. Leave to soak for 30 minutes,
to allow the milk to soak into the bread.

Heat the oven at 170°C/325°F/gas 3–4. Bake pud in the
moderate oven for 40–45 minutes until the top is golden
brown and crispy.

To serve: Put pud into a low oven (170°C/325°F/gas 3–4)
for 5–10 minutes while eating the main course. Serve on
its own or with pouring cream.

APPLE TART

Add a few blackberries or raspberries when in season.
Another masculine favourite – just like mother makes! A
good dessert to serve in addition to the cheeseboard.
Make in advance, warm through and serve with cream or
ice-cream.

Preparation and cooking time: 50–60 mins.

8 oz/250g shortcrust pastry – see page 145 or 1 small
**   packet frozen shortcrust pastry**
1 lb/500g cooking apples

(continued overleaf)

(Apple Tart continued)

3–4 oz/75–100g sugar, according to taste
Little milk for brushing
1 tblsp sugar – white or brown – for topping

Heat the oven at 200°C/400°F/gas 6–7. Make pastry, divide dough in half and roll out one piece thinly (¼"/½cm), large enough to cover base of a 10"/25cm pie plate. Carefully lift pastry over rolling pin and fit it into the shape of the plate. Trim off extra pastry with a knife.

Peel, core and slice apples, slice thinly and arrange on pastry base. Pick over blackberries or raspberries if used and sprinkle on top of apples. Sprinkle sugar over fruit. Roll out rest of pastry as before, making a circle large enough to fit over the mound of fruit. Brush pastry round rim of dish with milk, lift pastry lid carefully over rolling pin and fit on top of pie, – do not stretch it, ease it into shape. Trim off excess pastry. Pinch edges together and "knock up" edges with a knife. Brush top of pie with milk, sprinkle with sugar and make a tiny hole in centre of crust to let the steam escape.

Bake in the hot oven for 20–30 minutes until a light golden colour. Put aside until needed, or freeze and defrost overnight before serving.

To serve warm, put pie into a very low oven (150°C/300°F/gas 2–3) when serving the main course.

Serve cream or ice-cream separately.

SUNSHINE PIE   🟦   or   ◑   ❄

Sounds more interesting than treacle tart! I had to include this recipe as I've not met a man yet who doesn't appear enthusiastic when treacle tart is mentioned. Best served just warmed.

Preparation and cooking time: 30 mins.

**4 oz/125g quantity shortcrust pastry (see page 145) or
    ½ small packet frozen shortcrust pastry
2–3 handfuls cornflakes
6 heaped tblsp (approx.) golden syrup**

Heat the oven at 200°C/400°F/gas 6–7. Make pastry (see page 145) or defrost frozen pastry. Roll pastry out thinly (¼"/½cm), lift it carefully over the rolling pin and line a 10"/25cm pie plate, pressing it gently to fit the shape of the plate. Trim edges and decorate edges to make a sun (make cuts all round rim of pastry at 1"/2½cm intervals, damp pastry edge and turn the little squares over to make points, press together and knock up with a knife).

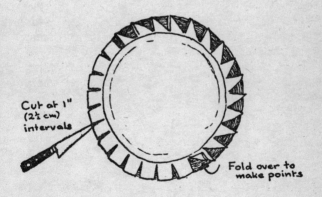

Cut at 1"
(2½ cm)
intervals

Fold over to
make points

Fig. 3. Sunshine Pie

Cover pastry hollow with slightly crushed cornflakes and spoon syrup over the top, covering cornflakes completely.

Bake in the hot oven for 8–10 minutes – remove from oven as soon as edges are very lightly coloured.

To serve: Warm through slightly in a very low oven (100°C/225°F/gas ½–1) while you are eating the main course. Thick cream or Greek yoghurt can be served at the table separately. Can be frozen after baking, defrost for 1–2 hours and warm through to serve.

11   DREAMY DESSERTS

Wicked but wonderful! Be extravagant: if you're going to serve cream at all, serve lots of it! Serve pouring cream in a large jug, or whip double cream until thick but not stiff and buttery, and tempt your guests with a beautiful bowl of thick cream to ladle over their dessert, or serve a bowl of Greek yoghurt if you're more health-conscious, or crème fraiche.

Make your own puds, or cheat and buy a really exotic fresh or frozen dessert, the choice is mouth-watering. If you're offering a choice of puds, make sure you have enough to go round when everyone wants a taste of all of them, and serve contrasting types of desserts – a creamy mousse, a cheesecake and a fruit tart for example, will look good and taste delicious.

Don't forget the cheese board, before or after the dessert (depending on nationality), or perfectly accept-

able on its own, followed by coffee and perhaps some
extravagant mint chocolates.

ICE-CREAM WITH CHOCOLATE FUDGE SAUCE [V] [S] [LM]

Choose any ice-cream to suit your taste and pocket –
plain vanilla, chocolate or coffee, or go for one of the
super American flavours, toffee with almond, mint chip,
etc. To be really rash you can even have 2 or 3 different
flavours!! The sauce can be made beforehand and
reheated while you eat the main course.

Preparation and cooking time: 10 mins.

Chocolate fudge sauce – see page 156
1 litre-size container of ice-cream
To serve: ½ pint/280ml carton double cream
6 tsp chopped nuts and/or chocolate 'sprinkles'
1 packet 'posh' wafer biscuits

Make chocolate fudge sauce – see page 156.
To serve: Put pyrex jug of sauce into a pan with 2"/5cm
very gently simmering water, and leave over a low heat
while eating the main course.

Put 2 or 3 scoops of chosen ice-cream in sundae dishes
or large wine glasses, pour over the fudge sauce and top
with a spoonful of cream. Decorate with a sprinkle of nuts
and/or chocolate 'sprinkles', and stick a wafer biscuit in
the side. Serve at once.

TANGERINE DESSERT [V] [S]

Use any of the lovely sweet seedless tangerine-type

oranges in season – mandarins, satsumas, clementines, etc., or use sweet dessert oranges if you prefer.

Preparation time: 15 mins. Chilling time: 2 hours or overnight.

Allow 2 tangerines or 1 large orange per person
Syrup – 6 oz/150g sugar
       ½ pint/⅓ litre orange juice
       2–3 tblsp orange liqueur – Cointreau, Curaçao
       or Grand Marnier (you can use a miniature bottle)
To serve: ½ pint/300ml thick cream or crème fraiche
      (optional)

Wash chosen fruit well and grate orange-coloured zest into a bowl. Peel fruit, scrape away any white pith and put into a deep serving dish.

Make syrup: Put sugar and orange juice into a pan and heat gently over a moderate heat, stirring occasionally until the sugar has dissolved, then allow it to boil gently for 5 minutes to produce a syrup. Remove from heat, stir in liqueur and grated orange peel. Allow to cool slightly, then pour warm syrup over fruit in dish and allow to cool.

Cover and chill in fridge for at least 2 hours or preferably overnight, occasionally spooning syrup over the fruit to allow it to soak up the flavour.

Serve cold, with cream or crème fraiche if liked.

FRESH STRAWBERRIES   Ⓥ   Ⓢ

Served at the beginning of the English strawberry season, a *huge* bowl of beautiful English strawberries is always popular – but it must be a big bowlful or it doesn't look spectacular enough.

Preparation time: 5 mins.

At least 2 lb/1kg strawberries
Bowl of sugar – there's always someone who likes it
Approx. 1 pint/600ml thick double cream or crème fraiche
Fresh mint or lemon balm leaves to decorate

Rinse, drain and hull strawberries, place in a large serving bowl, cover with plastic film and keep cool until needed – they have more flavour if not iced in the fridge. Serve with a large bowl of chosen cream, and decorate with leaves of mint or lemon balm. It also looks very effective just to rinse the strawberries and place in the bowl with the stalks still on. Serve as an 'extra' pud or with the cheeseboard – guests help themselves to the fruit and eat them with their fingers – don't forget the sugar, but you won't need cream.

BRANDY SNAPS WITH FRESH CREAM $\boxed{\frac{\mho}{V}}$ $\boxed{S}$ $\boxed{L^M}$

No one will mind if you cheat with this pud, it's so delicious. Prepare at the last minute, but whip the cream and put serving dishes ready beforehand.

Preparation time: 5 mins.

12 large brandy snaps – buy in packets from
**   the supermarket or baker's shop**
½ pint/280ml carton double cream or spooning cream or
**   use cream from an aerosol can**

Fill brandy snaps after the main course, as they go soggy if left standing very long, especially if using the aerosol cream. Whip double cream until really thick and store in fridge until needed. When ready to eat, fill each end of each brandy snap with cream; it's easier using the handle of a spoon, or squirt aerosol cream decoratively into each end. Arrange attractively on a large plate and serve.

RASPBERRY OR STRAWBERRY CREAM

This must be the ultimate in simple but delicious puds – buy the fruit and cream on your way home and the sweet is ready for table in 5 minutes.

Preparation time: 5 mins.

2 lb/1kg fresh ripe raspberries or strawberries
1 pint/600ml double cream or Greek yoghurt – or a mixture according to taste (cream on its own is super!)
2–4 oz/50–100g caster sugar (if needed)
Mint leaves to decorate

Rinse fruit and hull strawberries, pick fruit over well. Save a few berries for decoration and mash the rest of the fruit gently with a fork – don't crush too much. Sweeten to taste if necessary.

Whip cream until thick but not solid, mix in Greek yoghurt if used and fold fruit into cream mixture. Pour into a large glass dish and chill in fridge until needed. Decorate with mint leaves and serve.

EXOTIC FRUIT SALAD

Anyone can make a fruit salad, and it's always very

popular, but if you're making one for a dinner party it's
got to be a spectacular one!

Preparation time: 20–30 mins.   Chilling time: 1–2 hours.

1 large or 2 medium Honeydew melons
A mixture of exotic fruits in season, choose fruits
**   which look pretty and are a little bit special:–**
½ lb/250g strawberries
3 kiwi fruit
¼ lb/125g green grapes
¼ lb/125g black grapes
1 small fresh pineapple
2–3 large fresh peaches or nectarines
You won't need all these, choose your own favourites,
**   I think just strawberries and kiwi fruit mixed with**
**   the fresh melon is absolutely delicious!**
¼–½ pint/approx ¼ litre fresh orange juice
To serve: **½ pint/284ml thick cream or**
**   Greek yoghurt or crème fraiche**

Wash and dry melon, cut off the top, about three-
quarters of the way up the fruit, using a pretty zig-zag cut.
Remove seeds from both pieces and scoop out the melon
flesh, leaving enough fruit inside to give a firm melon
shell. Cut melon fruit into bite-sized chunks and put into a
large bowl.

Prepare chosen fruit:–
Strawberries – wash and hull, leave small strawberries
whole, cut large ones in half.
Kiwi fruit – peel and cut into thin slices.
Grapes – wash, leave whole if seedless, or cut in half and
remove pips.
Pineapple – cut off top and bottom, remove rest of skin by
slicing downwards. Cut into rings, remove core, and cut

fruit into small chunks.

Peaches or Nectarines – wash and dry, do not peel. Cut in half, remove stones and cut each half into slices.

Add fruit (and any juices) to melon chunks in the bowl and mix gently, adding enough fresh orange juice to provide a little syrup. Cover and chill until needed.

To serve: Stand the melon half on a serving dish, pile the chilled fruit salad carefully into the melon – it should be piled above the rim – and serve at once. Hand round thick cream, or Greek yoghurt if liked, separately at the table.

APPLE SNOW   ⏷

Amazingly cheap (especially in the autumn when people are giving away windfalls!), very light and delicious, and popular with people who don't like cream. Make the same day (it separates if left overnight).

Preparation and cooking time: 25–30 mins.

2–2½ lb/1kg approx. cooking apples
3–4 tblsp water and juice of ½ lemon/1 tblsp lemon juice
4–8 oz/100–250g sugar
4 egg whites

Peel and core apples, slice thinly and simmer gently in a pan with the water and lemon juice until soft. Cool slightly, then purée in a processor or liquidizer or mash with a fork. Sweeten to taste.

Whip egg whites until stiff, and fold into apple purée, being careful not to burst the air bubbles. Pile into a serving bowl and chill until needed. For a more exotic taste, omit the lemon juice and cook the apples in white wine or cider instead of water.

GOOSEBERRY FOOL 🔲 🅂

We know someone who didn't like gooseberries until he tried this pud – then he ate three helpings and pronounced it delicious.

Preparation and cooking time: 30 mins.

2 lb/1kg gooseberries
3–4 tblsp water
4–8 oz/100–250g sugar to taste
1 pint/600ml double cream (use 2 large cartons)
To serve: small packet shortbread biscuits

Wash gooseberries, (no need to top and tail), and put into a large pan with the water. Simmer gently over a low heat for 8–10 minutes until soft, stirring occasionally. Cool slightly, then pour into liquidizer or processor and blend for a few moments, then sieve to give a velvety smooth purée. Sweeten to taste. Whip cream lightly until thick but not solid, and fold it into the fruit purée. Pour into a large serving dish and chill until needed. Serve with shortbread biscuits.

CREAMY CITRUS CHEESECAKE 🔲 ❋

Choose your favourite flavour – orange or lemon (or a mixture) or a really sharp grapefruit tang. Make in a loose-bottomed flan or cake tin, as it's rather delicate to decant.

Can be frozen in advance and defrosted to serve.

Preparation time: 15 mins.   Setting time: 1 hour.

Base: **6 oz/150g/12 digestive biscuits**
       3 oz/75g butter
       2 oz/50g demerara sugar
Topping: **6 oz/150g cream cheese**
          1 lemon and/or 1 orange or 1 large grapefruit
          1–2 tblsp sugar to taste
          ¾ pint/450ml double cream
To decorate: **Lemon or orange twists or a few
    fresh strawberries or raspberries**

Make base: Put biscuits into a large bowl and crush with
end of a rolling pin. Melt butter gently in a largish
saucepan (do not let it boil and brown) and stir in sugar
and biscuit crumbs. Lightly butter the *base* of a 9″/22cm
loose-bottomed tin and spoon mixture into tin to make a
flat, even base.
Topping: Put cream cheese into a basin. Wash chosen
fruit thoroughly and grate rind into cheese, squeeze juice,
mix in 2–3 tblsp with a little sugar to taste. Whip cream
until stiff and fold into cheese mixture. Spoon on top of
base and leave in fridge or open freeze and defrost for 3–4
hours before use. Serve decorated with citrus twists (cut
thin circles of orange or lemon, cut through to the centre
and twist), or decorate with a few fresh strawberries or
raspberries.

MUM'S CHOCOLATE MOUSSE ⏣

You can add a little alcohol to this recipe (rum or sherry
are suitable) or add some orange juice, but we think it's
good enough on its own. It's a bit fiddly to make (takes
lots of basins), but it can be made in advance. Serve with
'posh' wafer biscuit rolls. You need a mixer for this recipe.

Preparation time: 20 mins.

8 oz/250g cooking chocolate – preferably plain
6 eggs
1 small wine glass of sherry or rum } **optional**
or juice of 1 orange
Serve with – ½ pint (300ml) thick double cream, Greek
    yoghurt or crème fraiche
Small packet wafer rolls
6 tsp chopped nuts – optional

Put chocolate in a pyrex jug or basin (not metal or plastic, it gets too hot), and stand jug in a pan with water a third of the way up the basin. Simmer water gently until chocolate melts (do not let it get too hot or the chocolate goes solid again). Separate eggs, put yolks into a small basin and whites in a large one. Beat egg whites until stiff but not dry, then beat egg yolks until really runny (you need not wash the beaters doing it this way round).

When chocolate has melted, remove from pan and beat in egg yolks and rum, sherry or orange juice if used. Very carefully, using a metal spoon, fold in beaten egg, mixing gently so as not to burst the air bubbles. Spoon into small glasses or sundae dishes and chill until needed.

To serve: Sprinkle a few chopped nuts on top of each mousse, decorate with a wafer roll and hand cream or Greek yoghurt separately.

CRUNCHY APPLE AND BLACKBERRY ICE-CREAM ⏏ ❄

This is delicious and looks really pretty, two different mousses frozen together. Make well in advance and freeze, defrosting for about 1 hour before eating. You need a mixer or processor for this recipe.

Preparation time: 30 mins.
Freezing time: approx. 2 hours.

Apple Mousse:	*Blackberry Mousse:*
1½ lb/750g cooking apples	½ lb/250g blackberries
3–4 tblsp water	1–2 tblsp water
2 egg whites	2–3 oz/50–75g sugar
4–6 oz/100–150g sugar	1 egg white
¾ pint/425ml double cream	¼ pint/150ml double cream

6–8 unfilled meringue shells
Keep the two fruits separate

Peel and core cooking apples, cut into thin slices and simmer gently with a little water for 5–10 minutes until soft. Blend in processor or liquidizer for a few seconds, then sieve to give a smooth purée. Sweeten to taste.

Wash blackberries, cook and blend as above to produce a smooth purée. Sweeten to taste.

Whip all three egg whites together until thick and fold two-thirds into the apple and one third into the blackberry. Whip all the cream (use the same bowl, less washing-up) until thick but not solid, and fold three-quarters into the apple and a quarter into the blackberry. Pour each mousse into a shallow plastic box (old ice-cream cartons are useful), and freeze for about an hour until half frozen. Remove from freezer and beat each mousse well until mushy. Crush meringue shells slightly and mix them into the blackberry mush. Then, using a metal spoon, carefully fold the blackberry mousse into the apple mousse, giving a ripple effect. Pour fruit mixture into one plastic tub and freeze until needed.

To serve: Defrost ice-cream in the fridge for about half an hour – take it from the freezer before serving the main course. Serve scoops of ice-cream in pretty glass dishes.

LEMON SYLLABUB   🖭

Very delicious! Very rich! Serve syllabub in stemmed wine glasses and serve shortbread biscuits separately on the table. Prepare the same day and chill in fridge until needed. You need a mixer for this recipe.

Preparation time: 15 mins.   Chilling time: 2 hours.

2 egg whites
4 oz/100g caster sugar
Juice of 1 lemon or 2 tblsp lemon juice
1 wine-glass white wine or dry sherry
½ pt/284ml carton double cream
1 lemon for decoration

Beat the egg whites until stiff, beat in sugar a spoonful at a time, then gradually whip in lemon juice and wine or sherry. Whip cream until thick but still runny and pour into the syllabub mixture. Continue beating until the syllabub is smooth and thick. Pour into 6 large wine glasses and chill in fridge. Make lemon twists for decoration – cut 6 thin rounds of lemon, cut nearly through to the centre, and twist.
To serve: Put a twist of lemon on top of each syllabub, stand glass on a side plate and serve with a shortbread biscuit.

TIM'S CRÈME BRÛLÉE   🖭

My very favourite dessert, expensive but gorgeous. The crème must be prepared the day before to give it time to set completely. The brûlée part only takes five minutes, but has to be done no more than 2 or 3 hours before dinner or it will not stay crisp. Do serve it really cold to give the lovely cold, creamy flavour.

Preparation and cooking time: Crème – 35–40 mins.
  (must be made the day before).
Brûlée: 5 mins.

Crème: **6 eggs**
3 heaped tblsp sugar
1½ pints/900ml single or whipping cream (check the
  amount in the cartons of cream)
½ tsp vanilla essence

Brûlée Topping: **6–8 tblsp demerara sugar**

This will fill 6–8 ramekins according to size.

Heat the oven at 150°C/300°F/gas 2–3. Make crème –
beat eggs and sugar together gently (use a whisk or a
fork). Mix in cream and vanilla essence. Pour into
ramekin dishes, stand these in a deep tin or large
ovenproof dish, pour about 1″/2½cm hot water into the
dish, enough to come only halfway up the ramekins, and
bake for 25–30 minutes, until just firm. Allow to cool,
then leave in fridge overnight.
  2–3 hours before serving heat grill until really hot.
  Cover top of each crème completely with a layer of
demerara sugar, place on grill pan close to the grill, and
brown for 1–2 minutes, until the sugar has melted and
turned crispy – it may be necessary to change the dishes
around to brown them evenly – and the top is a deep
golden brown colour. Allow to cool, then chill in fridge
until ready to eat.

CHEESE AND FRUIT BOARD 🍇 Ⓢ

This is easy to prepare, and it's very pleasant to sit round the table and talk, nibble at the cheese and drink coffee at the end of an enjoyable meal. It also 'pads out' the pud, although it's certainly not always necessary to serve a dessert, and cheese is quite acceptable instead. You don't have to provide a choice of a dozen different cheeses either (you're not running a restaurant), one or two 'special' cheeses such as a large slab of creamy Brie, a small Camembert or a nice ripe piece of Stilton or other blue cheese, with a good piece of Cheddar or Double Gloucester or Creamy Walnut for the less adventurous, is quite adequate.

Brighten up the cheese board with a bunch of rinsed grapes, a bowl of walnuts or a jug of lovely crisp celery. Serve with bread or biscuits – digestives, water biscuits, cream crackers or a box of 'mixed biscuits for cheese' and butter.

12 ODDS AND ENDS

All the recipes for sauces and accompaniments which everyone assumes they know, but are useful to have to hand if only for the amounts to use.

SHORTCRUST PASTRY

Do not under any circumstances have your first attempt at making pastry on the day of your dinner party! Have a practice beforehand, or use frozen pastry.

Preparation time: 10 mins.

To make ½ lb/250g shortcrust pastry (you measure pastry by the amount of flour used in the recipe):

½ lb/250g plain flour (self raising flour gives a puddingy
   result)
¼ tsp salt
4 oz/125g butter, margarine, lard or vegetable fat –
   I prefer to use a half and half mixture of butter
   and white fat, butter for colour and flavour, white
   fat for texture; do not use lard if you are
   feeding a vegetarian.
Approx. 8 tsp cold water
A little extra flour for rolling out

Sieve flour and salt into a bowl. Add chosen fat cut into
small pieces. Using tips of your fingers, rub in flour and
fat to form 'breadcrumbs'. Add the cold water gradually,
mixing in with a knife and then using fingertips to form
into a lump of dough – don't get pastry too wet (add a
little extra flour if it's too sticky) and handle as little as
possible to get a lovely light pastry when cooked. The
pastry is now ready to roll out on a lightly floured
worktop. It can be wrapped in plastic film and left in the
fridge until needed.

GARLIC AND HERB BREAD

Always popular, especially tempting to those who are
slimming, because it smells so good! Make in advance and
freeze uncooked, defrost before heating, or put aside and
pop into the hot oven just before eating.

Preparation time: 10 mins.   Heating time: 5–10 mins.

You will need 1–2 French loaves between six people,
depending on appetite and the size of the loaves. For one
average-sized French loaf use:

1–2 cloves garlic or 1 tsp garlic powder or paste
4 oz/100g butter
Handful of fresh herbs, parsley, chives, etc. (optional)
1 long French loaf and large piece of foil for wrapping

Peel, chop and crush fresh garlic until smooth, then beat together with the butter until soft and creamy; it's easier if the butter is softened to start with. Beat in washed, finely snipped herbs.

Check that the loaf will fit in the oven, if not cut it in half and make two parcels. Cut loaf nearly through into 1″/2½cm slices (be careful not to cut slices right through or the loaf will drop to bits) and butter between the slices generously on both sides with garlic butter. Press loaf together again and wrap loosely in kitchen foil. Put aside or freeze until needed. Before baking, defrost for 1 to 2 hours, according to size.

To serve, heat oven at 200°C/400°F/gas 6–7, and bake the foil-wrapped loaf for 5–10 minutes according to size, until crisp and hot right through. Unfold and serve at once.

MIX 'N MATCH STUFFING

Sage and onion is traditionally served with pork; thyme and parsley with chicken or turkey, but any herby mixture is tasty.

Preparation and cooking time: 45 mins.

1 large onion (optional)
2–3 slices bread – white or brown
1 packet (3 oz/75g size) stuffing mix, flavour to taste
1 tblsp mixed herbs

(continued overleaf)

(Mix 'n Match Stuffing continued)

1 tblsp lemon juice – optional
Hot water to mix
1 oz/25g butter

Peel and chop onion (omit this for thyme and parsley if preferred), put onion into a saucepan with 1 cup/5 fl oz/150ml hot water, bring to the boil and simmer for 5–10 minutes until softened. Make breadcrumbs – use a grater or blender. Remove onion from heat and stir in the chosen stuffing mix, breadcrumbs, herbs and lemon juice, (if not using onion, mix dry ingredients with hot water from the kettle and lemon juice), adding extra hot water if needed to make a stiff mixture. Well grease an ovenproof dish, put stuffing into dish, dot with butter and put aside until needed.

Bake for 30–40 minutes in a hot oven (200°C/400°F/gas 6–7), timed to be ready with the main course, or cook a little earlier and keep warm if necessary.

CROÛTONS 📓

Delicious additions to hot, cream soups. You only need a few to sprinkle on top of each serving. Can be made in advance, drained on kitchen paper and put aside until needed.

Preparation time: 10 mins.

Enough for 6 generous helpings
3 slices bread – white or brown
1–2 tblsp vegetable oil
1–2 oz/25–50g butter

Cut crusts off bread and cut into ½"/1cm cubes. Heat oil

and butter in a large frying pan over a moderate heat, add bread cubes and fry for 2–3 minutes, turning frequently with a fish slice until the cubes are golden and crispy on all sides – be careful not to get the fat too hot and smoking. Remove croûtons from pan and drain well on kitchen paper.

To serve, sprinkle a few croûtons on top of each bowl of soup, or serve separately at the table.

GRAVY   🔥   S

The meat juices from the roasting tin can be used on their own as a sauce, poured over the meat, but if you want 'proper' gravy, remember that the more flour you use, the thicker the gravy. The liquid used can be any mixture of water, vegetable water (think of all those vitamins!), wine, sherry, beer or cider. You can use prepared gravy granules if you wish, mixed with hot water as instructed on the packet, adding any meat juices from the tin.

Preparation and cooking time: 5 mins.

Medium gravy for 6 people
1 tblsp flour or cornflour
1–2 tsp gravy powder
1 stock cube – use appropriate flavour for the meat
1 pint/600ml approx. water, veg water and/or wine,
    sherry, beer or cider
Any juices from the meat tin

Mix flour or cornflour and gravy powder with a little of the liquid to make a smooth paste. Add crumbled stock cube and rest of the liquid, and the juices from the roasting tin. Mix well. Pour into a saucepan and bring to the boil, stirring all the time, adding a little more liquid if gravy is too thick, or mix up a little more cornflour with cold water and stir into gravy if the sauce is too thin.

To thicken gravy in stews and casseroles, make gravy mix as above, omitting stock cube, and stir the runny mixture into the casserole. Bring back to the boil, stirring gently, so that the gravy thickens as it cooks.

WHITE SAUCE

A basic savoury sauce, add other ingredients as required. I think that this is the easiest method of making a white sauce; although it may be frowned on by the purists, it works!

Preparation and cooking time: 10 mins.

2 oz/50g/2 tblsp cornflour
1 pint/600ml milk
2 oz/50g butter or margarine
Salt, black pepper

Put cornflour into a basin and mix to a smooth paste with a little of the milk. Boil rest of milk, stir flour mixture again, and pour milk into flour mixture, stirring well. Pour milk mixture back into pan, return to the heat and bring back to the boil, stirring all the time, until sauce thickens. Beat in butter or margarine, and season well with salt and black pepper. Serve hot.

CHEESE SAUCE: Grate 6–8 oz/150–250g Cheddar cheese and beat into the sauce with the butter or marg., and add 1 tsp mustard with the seasoning, (mature Cheddar will give the best 'cheesy' flavour).

PARSLEY SAUCE: Wash and drain a large handful of fresh parsley, and snip the sprigs into the sauce with the seasoning.

ITALIAN TOMATO SAUCE

Blend this super spicy sauce in a processor or liquidizer to get a really smooth result, although it can be used without blending if you prefer. It's delicious with pasta of all kinds, or poured over vegetables, or served with meat dishes instead of gravy.

Preparation and cooking time: 30–35 mins.
Makes 1 pint/600ml approx.

2 large onions
2 cloves garlic or ½ tsp ground garlic
2 tblsp oil for frying (olive oil gives a good flavour)
14 oz/398g can peeled Italian tomatoes or 1 lb fresh,
ripe tomatoes
2 tblsp tomato purée or ketchup
1–2 dried Italian tomatoes in oil (optional, buy from
delicatessens; they give a lovely flavour)
1 tsp sugar
1 tsp mixed herbs
Salt, black pepper, Worcester sauce

Peel and finely chop onions, peel and chop or crush garlic. Heat oil in a saucepan over a moderate heat, and fry onion and garlic gently for 4–5 minutes until soft but not browned. Break up canned or wash and chop fresh tomatoes, and add to the onion. Stir in tomato purée or ketchup, finely chopped dried tomatoes, sugar, and herbs. Season to taste with salt, black pepper and Worcester sauce. Bring to the boil, stirring well, then reduce heat, cover and simmer for 10–15 minutes, stirring occasionally, until soft and 'saucy'. Allow to cool slightly, then blend in a liquidizer or processor to make a smooth sauce. Put aside or freeze until needed.

Reheat when required, over a low heat, and pour over pasta, meat or vegetables, or serve separately in a sauceboat.

APPLE SAUCE   🔥 S ❄ 🏮

It was traditional in my husband's family to serve this with chicken as well as pork, so we still do, and it's very tasty.

Preparation and cooking time: 15 mins.

1–1½ lb/500–600g cooking apples
¼ pint/150ml/1 cup water
2–4 oz/50–100g sugar

Peel, core and thinly slice apples. Put into a saucepan with the water, bring to the boil, then simmer gently for 5–10 minutes, until the apples are soft – do not let the pan boil dry. Mash sauce with a fork until smooth (watch out for hot splashes), and sweeten to taste. Pour into a serving jug, and serve hot or cold. Can be made in advance, or frozen and defrosted overnight before reheating.

MINT SAUCE   👤 S 🏮

Traditionally served with lamb. Use fresh mint if you have it, or re-mix 'bought mint sauce'.

'Fresh' Mint Sauce

Large bunch fresh mint
2–3 tblsp vinegar
2–3 tsp sugar

Strip leaves from stalks, and wash, drain and chop or

process finely – it's much easier if you have a blender. Mix mint, vinegar and sugar together to taste, making a thick, runny sauce. Serve in a sauce-boat or jug. Can be made in advance and kept in a covered jar in the fridge.

'Bought' Mint Sauce

1 jar mint sauce
1–2 tblsp vinegar
2–3 tsp sugar

Mix mint, vinegar and sugar to taste, and serve as above.

TIM'S YOGHURT AND CUCUMBER SAUCE ⓥ Ⓢ 🌶

Men seem to enjoy making sauces! This is a lovely one to serve with hot chilli or curry. Make in advance and store in the fridge.

Preparation time: 5 mins.

½ pint/300ml/1 large tub plain or chive-flavoured yoghurt
   (low fat or Greek type)
½ cucumber
1–2 tblsp lemon juice to taste
Salt, black pepper

Put yoghurt into a basin. Wash cucumber and cut into tiny (¼"/½cm) dice, and stir into yoghurt. Stir in lemon juice to taste and season with salt and black pepper. Pour into a serving bowl and hand separately.

AVOCADO SAUCE OR DIP 🌀 S 📷

A very pretty-coloured sauce; a good substitute for home-made mayonnaise if you're worried about using raw eggs. To use as a dip, stir in less yoghurt or cream to give a thicker consistency. Very soft or over-ripe avocados can be used in this recipe (often sold off cheaply in the supermarket).

Preparation time: 5 mins.

2 large soft avocado pears
1 tub/5 fl oz/142ml plain yoghurt
1 tub/5 fl oz/142ml soured cream, double cream or crème
  fraiche
Few sprigs fresh chives and/or parsley
2–3 tsp lemon juice – to taste
Salt, black pepper

Peel avocados, remove stones. Chop fruit into a basin and mash to a pulp with a fork. Blend in yoghurt and chosen cream (any mixture according to taste and pocket) to make a good coating "cream". If making a dip, just add enough yoghurt or cream to give thick "dip" consistency. Wash and finely scissor-snip herbs into sauce. Season to taste with lemon juice, salt and black pepper. This sauce is good with salads, or poured over hot green vegetables – asparagus, broccoli, mangetout peas, French beans, etc.

VINAIGRETTE (FRENCH) DRESSING 🌀

An essential sauce to have ready in the fridge. Make and store in a screw-top jar; it keeps for weeks and is the most widely used dressing for all types of salads. Quick and easy to make, and you can vary the basic recipe with your favourite flavourings – use herb vinegars or lemon juice, add a pinch of garlic or herbs, or use honey instead of sugar. Olive or walnut oils are expensive but give a beautiful flavour if you can afford to use them.

To make a jarful
Use proportions of 2 lots of oil to 1 lot of vinegar. Take a clean, screw-top jar or wide-necked bottle and pour into it:

1 cup/5 fl oz/150ml olive oil or vegetable oil
½ cup/2½ fl oz/70ml vinegar or lemon juice
¼ tsp salt
¼ tsp pepper
½ tsp mustard
1 tsp sugar

Screw lid on firmly and shake well for 2–3 minutes until thoroughly mixed. Store in the fridge and shake again before use. If it solidifies, stand the jar in warm water for a few minutes, or remove jar from fridge and stand in a warm room for half an hour, until dressing is runny again.

Add any flavourings when you mix the ingredients. Wine or herb vinegars have a less harsh flavour than malt vinegar.

YOGHURT DRESSING

A really tangy sauce. Use as a salad dressing or pour over hot vegetables – cauliflower, broccoli or carrots.

Preparation time: 5 mins.

Makes ½ pint/300ml sauce

2 small tubs/½ pint/300ml plain yoghurt – low fat or Greek
Juice of 1 lemon – 2 tblsp lemon juice
1–2 tsp runny honey
Few sprigs fresh parsley or chives
Salt and black pepper

Put yoghurt into a basin. Stir in lemon juice and honey and mix well. Stir in washed, snipped herbs and season with salt and pepper.

Yoghurt flavoured with chives is good in this recipe. A tub of plain yoghurt poured over hot vegetables or salad makes an instant sauce when you're in a hurry.

CHOCOLATE FUDGE SAUCE   H   S

A smooth chocolaty sauce. Use whichever kind of chocolate you prefer to make a delicious topping for ice-cream.

Preparation and cooking time: 10 mins.

10 oz/300g chocolate chips, choc cake covering, cooking
**   chocolate or chocolate bars, e.g. Mars bars**
4 heaped tblsp brown sugar
4 tblsp cold water
4 oz/100g butter (preferably unsalted)
2 tblsp rum or orange juice (optional)

Put chosen chocolate, sugar and water into a small pan over a very low heat and stir well until the choc melts, making a smooth, creamy mixture. Remove from heat, cut butter into pieces and beat into the sauce. Beat in rum or orange if used. Pour over ice-cream.

If reheating later, pour into a pyrex jug, and warm through when needed by standing the jug in 2"/5cm hot water in a pan over a very low heat. Simmer gently until sauce is melted, stir and serve.

INDEX